Amelia Rosselli

Document

translated from Italian by
Roberta Antognini and Deborah Woodard

with an afterword and notes by Roberta Antognini

 WORLD POETRY

Document by Amelia Rosselli
© Garzanti Editore s.p.a., 1997
© 2004, 2016, Garzanti s.r.l., Milano
Gruppo editoriale Mauri Spagnol

English translation copyright © Roberta Antognini & Deborah Woodard, 2025
Afterword and Notes to the Poems copyright © Roberta Antognini, 2025

Originally published in 1976 as *Documento* (1966-1973) by Garzanti, Milan.

First Edition, First Printing, 2025
ISBN 978-1-954218-29-1

World Poetry Books
New York, NY
www.worldpoetrybooks.com

Available to the trade through Asterism Books
Distributed in the UK and Europe by Turnaround Publisher Services
Subscriptions and standing orders available directly from the publisher

Library of Congress Control Number: 2025930682

Cover design by Andrew Bourne
Typesetting by Don't Look Now
Printed in Lithuania by BALTO Print

World Poetry Books is a 501(c)(3) nonprofit and charitable organization founded in 2017 in New York City, affiliated with the Humanities Institute and the Translation Program at the University of Connecticut (Storrs), and a member of the Community of Literary Magazines and Presses (CLMP).

World Poetry's publications and programs are made possible with funding from the Poetry Foundation and the New York State Council on the Arts, as well as generous support from individual donors and subscribers. Additional support for this book was provided by a grant from the Mellon Career and Curricular Transitions Endowment Fund.

Table of Contents

Document
(1966–1973)

[just before I had to leave I wrote]	13
[I don't bring cheese with me: I write]	15
[Just because I show up you've got a pencil]	17
Insomnia	19
[Without even winning themselves over]	21
to Renato	23
[I'd like to give you all my blood.]	25
[Oxygen in my curtains, it's you,]	27
[Stones turn taut in the woods: they have little]	29
[With sickness in my mouth]	31
[A quick ruckus of muffled wings]	33
[I dreamed visits of relatives]	35
[The night was a splendid reed]	37
to Shubert	39
[I graft into living]	41
[This finding the way to your heart]	43
[Just the facts, repressing your feelings]	45
[Vaccination, my writing]	47
[Noticing me he realized he was]	49
[In the darkest hour I saw the sunset]	53
[Lamented paradise: peace on earth if]	55
[I saw the sky gloat: it was purple]	57
[If ever in my mind despair]	59
[Daughter of a devouring love did I]	61
[Concatenation of causes: you've seen the shadow]	63
[How many fields sponge-like would hope]	65
[How many branches have the olive groves]	67
[You're in my breast, but then I find you,]	69
[Forgive our faults as I forgive the terrors]	71
[And poison straining through occult nerves]	73
[The hard life of the executed renovated]	75
[Hand uninterrupted still guides impotence]	77
[You look for justice: you'll never find it]	79
[What action to choose, predict, inherit?]	81

[As long as it doesn't become vanity it's not liberty]	83
[Soft reverberation of the pillow made for]	85
[Psychologically dexterous the diamond]	87
[Love that divides us and unites us endures]	89
[Quick reflexes: save yourself]	91
[Love blue and green: what a breakdown I]	93
[As I approached the walls also odorous]	95
[A horror of shivering falling bombs]	97
[At the distilled dinners]	99
[Flowers arrive as a gift and then dilate]	101
[Provenance of *caoutchouc*]	103
[Twitchy sun awakens us from the long]	105
[with earth seeming to tremble from coincidences]	107
[a blue that's not even blue or anyway]	109
[Preset wires stretch from tree]	111
[How many dense and orgiastic stars]	113
Dialogue with the Dead	117
[They found white rags on the ground...]	121
[A blue blue blue blue blue sea, even green]	123
[Freedom to lose oneself in the split callus of]	125
[Counting the prisoners: their mouths]	127
[You weren't ready]	129
[Wind easterly and southwest of the mob]	131
[I dreamed of lust that has instead]	133
[Your dark forehead]	135
[In a tired and blue encounter]	137
[I distinguished between your death and mine;]	139
[A squared solitude,]	143
[I rhymed, toward a bank]	145
[Flanking the empty tree the ants']	147
[And I've seen syllables lifting me up]	151
[I raved, imperfect, on a ladder]	153
[Night, drawn labyrinth]	155
[Pines have sea nearby and warm sand]	157
[Ah how quiet are the blackbirds! They confused]	159
[Wind with slimy traces in a desert]	161
[Revolutionary tents in my heart]	163
[Flowers stripped and tuneless in the humble]	165
[Stable horses guarded by]	167
[And those kids have soft coats]	169

[Taking the employees with you]	171
[unacceptable reality]	173
[They melted the war device with my]	175
[It's]	179
[One face of yours has such human contours]	181
[this is the sea today]	183
[He too hanged the revolution]	185
[I've twenty days]	187
[That primary destroyed flow]	189
[Fire scales uncommon branches]	191
[Cold is scary and blood too]	193
[Verdigris-infused branch in accord with a]	195
[it mustn't fall and shatter]	197
Snow	199
[A thousand small, delicate objects, the]	201
Collapse	203
[Once more I meddled]	205
[You thought you could love me? You saw in me]	207
[It rings constantly; a deadly compromise]	209
[Strong in its ministerial]	211
[The tortured imagination tormented itself]	213
[In a hotel room, meditating upon]	215
[This game]	219
[This hate in others' faces]	221
Letter	223
[Still before a destiny ever self-moving]	225
[Listen]	227
[Such indolent conversations]	229
[We're in the desert's green shadow]	231
[A green or orange piece of paper I]	233
[while with your head on fire]	235
[Inclined birds on the sloped roofs]	237
[Efforts of splendid and empty freedom]	239
[Jealous of the space precluding,]	241
[My angel, I never knew which angel]	243
[The slippery heart so rebellious in me]	245
[Without you]	247
[Robust animal dung has]	249
[Victorious in nothing over nothing, the]	251
[Pointing fingers at the soil]	253

[Had it been easier sharing you,]	257
[It's a flame of will]	259
[Your indelible face on paper]	261
[Not this torture]	263
[The name bearer of this bizarre letter]	265
[Passion rightly devoured me]	267
[I propose an encounter with the skull,]	271
[Once the goal is achieved]	273
[Out of tune life,]	275
[lymphatic canals scented]	277
[Fan-shaped alibis]	279
Campagnano	281
[I've removed each light]	283
[Genuine genuflections—a rivalry]	285
[I rest my pate]	287
[Nobody]	289
[In imagination alone]	291
[that morning after secretly]	293
[So furiously wild]	295
[There's something like pain in the room, and]	297
[Backwards clouds]	299
[On the same pavement]	301
General Strike 1969	303
[Rose tidied up]	305
[Your white hands]	307
[Rivers in weariest tears]	309
[Sterilizations of reality]	311
[The angels are leaving]	313
[Of traitors]	315
[As if I knew what the opposite meant]	317
[Without a drop of beauty]	319
[If you must feed your blood]	321
[You too died; or wanted to die, I]	323
[Your exquisite confections console,]	325
[I left people lying about: my slippers]	327
[The reason for the storms: they've spread]	329
[In this desert of the spirit that inspires me]	333
[I try out a market—then I try another one]	335
[By now the dialogue is between two or three people]	339
[Your ash-blonde]	341

[It's simple love, this]	343
[If sinisterly, I saw you]	345
[the young, their roses]	349
[Support collar and dead run, spun]	351
[How like the stones I am with you!—how like the]	353
[Presuming to be entirely destroyed, do]	357
[It's not true that by running it stands out]	359
for Gianfranco	361
[Hunger huffed and was extreme, symptom]	365
[lemon hill: impeccable]	367
The Christ (Easter 1971)	369
[Peaceful words]	371
[Easy to do]	373
[In the black star of my destiny]	375
[European continence, if anything it came]	377
[You can't withstand this winter]	379
[in the nordic]	381
[feeling very close to]	383
Snow 1973	385
[And in the aqueduct]	387
[Corruption in yesterday's paper]	389
Afterword	393
Notes to the Poems	399
Bibliography	407
Acknowledgments	409

Documento
(1966-1973)

Document
(1966–1973)

PROPRIO PRIMA DI dover partire scrissi
perciò voltando il dorso alla promessa
cose molto belle che solo tu con la
tua faccia infantile da ragazzo costretto
ad esser fiero puoi indicarmi.

Sì, scrissi finalmente cose belle, tutte
per te – non v'era pubblico più disattento.

JUST BEFORE I had to leave I wrote
thereby turning my back on the promise
very beautiful things that only you with
your childish face of a boy forced
to be proud can show me.

Yes, in the end I wrote beautiful things, all of them
for you—no audience was more distracted.

Non porto il formaggio con me: scrivo
sui muri o sui tuoi pantaloni. Hai
nella riviera tua delle tasche gonfie
di biscottini pronti per la marmellata:
il mio credermi santa voltando la pagina
per raggiungere te che non m'interessi
più.

Come mai? Mi son ritrovata biscotto
anch'io e non vengo all'appuntamento
a leggere le tue cose probabilmente
scritte male come me.

I don't bring cheese with me: I write
on the walls or on your pants. You have
in your swollen riviera pockets
cookies ready for jam:
believing myself a saint by turning the page
to reach you who I don't care for
anymore.

How come? I've become a cookie
myself and I don't show up
to read your things probably
badly written like me.

Solo perché ci vengo hai una matita
per scrivere di orrori?

Solo perché non ci vengo hai una matita
per scrivere di me?

Hai calzoni? Ho verde saliva.
Non vedo più i santi.

JUST BECAUSE I show up you've got a pencil
to write down the horrors?

Just because I don't show up you've got a pencil
to write about me?

Do you have pants? I've got green saliva.
I no longer see the saints.

Insonnia

I miei occhi che non s'aprono, dal
sonno o dalla tortura, ed invece eccoti
qua, a scegliere un'altra via: la medicina
per non addormentarti.

I miei occhi sembrano pieni di sabbia
tanto ha fatto l'alba svegliandosi
e costretta a riparare guasti, ha lanciato
motivi d'appello; per non svegliarsi
ma invece sono le cinque ogni giorno

prima che la notte ti conosca in piedi
o assorto nel sonno.

Insomnia

My eyes that won't open, from
sleep or torture, and yet here you are,
choosing another way: medicine
so as not to fall asleep.

My eyes feel full of sand
so much had dawn done waking up
and forced to patch things up, launching
grounds for appeals; not to wake up
but instead it's five every day

before the night finds you on your feet
or lost in sleep.

SENZA VINCERE NEMMENO se stessi
e come potrebbe quando fucilato?

Fu fucilato e essi si ravvisarono
dopo la sua morte intestata al
voler rovinarsi da soli e con
l'aiuto degli altri. Gli altri!
perché seppero di lui?

Lo fucilarono mentre beveva, e
non aveva guanti. Risse e la persecuzione,
troppo tardi agli occhi degli
altri si salvò.

Without even winning themselves over
and how could they once he was shot?

He was shot and they recognized each other
after his death signed over to
wanting to ruin themselves
and with the help of others. The others!
why did they know about him?

They shot him while he was drinking, and
gloveless. Brawls and persecution,
too late in the eyes of the
others he saved himself.

a Renato

Imparare ad avere fiducia! Senza di
te non posso sentire nell'aria altro
che cialtroni.

Ridere non è sempre amaro... forse l'aria
scrive di magia, miracoli, distensioni
caratteri che urgono d'amore.

Verità che rinasci che insperato tumore
è questo che m'assale con te correndo
per vie tumultuose?

to Renato

Learning to have faith! Without
you I can't sense in the air other
than buffoons.

Laughter isn't always bitter... maybe the air
writes of magic, miracles, distension
characters urging love.

You truth reborn what unexpected tumor
is this that assails me running with you
through tumultuous streets?

VORREI DONARTI IL mio sangue tutto.
Ma esso corre in piccoli inestricabili
rivoletti, e non graffia la tua porta
d'entrata con abbastanza tenerezza
per tenerci a galla.

O forse sei qua ad accompagnarmi? Ne
ho perso le vie anch'io di questa tua
triste casa. Non vedo altro che luci
e tramonti che a me sembrano diabolici.

Hai rime intense per me, non posso
provvedere al caso che tramite questo
tuo essere re delle mie giornate.

I'D LIKE TO give you all my blood.
But it runs in small inextricable
rivulets, and doesn't scratch your front
door with enough tenderness
to keep us afloat.

Or maybe you're here to come with me? I
too lost my ways to your
sad house. I see nothing but lights
and sunsets that seem diabolical.

You've got potent rhymes for me, I can't
account for it other than by this,
your being king of my days.

OSSIGENO NELLE MIE tende, sei tu, a
graffiare la mia porta d'entrata, a
guarire il mio misterioso non andare
non potere andare in alcun modo con
gli altri. Come fai? Mi sorvegli e
nel passo che ci congiunge v'è sopratutto
quintessenza di Dio; il suo farneticare
se non proprio amore qualcosa di più
grande: il tuo corpo la tua mente e
i tuoi muscoli tutti affaticati: da
un messaggio che restò lì nel vuoto
come se ad ombra non portasse messaggio
augurale l'inquilino che sono io: tua
figlia, in una foresta pietrificata.

OXYGEN IN MY curtains, it's you,
scratching my front door,
healing my mysterious ungoing
unable to go in any way with
others. How do you do it? You guard me and
in the step that unites us there is above all
God's quintessence; his babbling
if not exactly love something
bigger: your body your mind and
your muscles so weary: from
a message that lingered in the void
like a greeting to a shadow that hadn't
been delivered by the dweller, who was me: your
daughter, in a petrified forest.

Pietre tese nel bosco; hanno piccoli
amici, le formiche ed altri animali
che non so riconoscere. Il vento non
spazza via il sasso, quelle fosse, quei
resti d'ombra, quel vivere di sogni
pesanti.

Resti nell'ombra: ho un cuore che scotta
e poi si sfalda per ingenuamente ricordarsi
di non morire.

Ho un cuore come quella foresta: tutta
sarcastica a volte, i suoi rami lordi
discendono sulla testa a pesarti.

Stones turn taut in the woods; they have little
friends, ants and other animals
that I don't recognize. The wind doesn't
sweep away the stone, those holes, those
remains of a shadow, that life of heavy
dreams.

Remains in the shadows: I've a burning heart
and then it crumbles naively remembering
not to die.

I've a heart like that forest: quite
sarcastic at times, its gross branches
fall on your head, weigh you down.

CON LA MALATTIA in bocca
spavento
per gli spaventapasseri
rose stinte e vi sono macchie sul muro
piccolissime nel granaio dei tuoi pensieri:
e con quale colore smetti di
dipingere?

Avevo trovato il mio proprio opposto.
Come lo divorai! Poi lo mangiai. E ne
fui divorata, in belle lettere.

E correre poi
al riparo mentre corrono anche certe
vecchie, all'orinatoio.

Poi smettono di correre.

WITH SICKNESS IN my mouth
scared
by the scarecrows
faded roses and there are stains on the wall
so small in the granary of your thoughts:
and with which color do you quit
painting?

I'd found my exact opposite.
How I devoured it! Then I ate it. And
I was devoured by it, in *belles lettres*.
And then running
for cover while certain old
ladies run too, to the urinal.

Then they quit running.

UNO STREPITARE SVELTO di ali smorzate
questo incesto non
si ha da fare.

Nel cavo della mano rimane
solo un fluorescente pensarsi?

Le scienze
naturali e colte
il mio grido di fanciulla senza colomba.

A QUICK RUCKUS of muffled wings
this incest shall not
take place.

In the hollow of the hand remains
only a fluorescent thinking?

The natural and
cultivated sciences
my cry of a girl without a dove.

HO SOGNATO VISITE di parenti
maldestre donne e sindacati
mi congiungo a chi vive più vivo di me
sviscerare le piante, emettere un grido.

Poi dimostrarsi inadatti alla causa
mentre balenano pidocchi
scrittore in povertà, la mente
disturbata da nonsensi.

Come una bestia le tue indulgenze, e
i cuscini affondavano comodamente
in una specie di clausola senza causa
senza emettere un suono.

Mentre fiaschi di vino e trappole usuali
strizzavano l'occhio a tanta verginità
ed ora annaspa nel retrocampo
umiliandosi le mani.

I DREAMED VISITS of relatives
clumsy women and unions
I join those who live more alive than I
eviscerating plants, emitting a cry.

Then proving yourself unequal
to the cause while lice flash
writer in poverty, the mind
disturbed by nonsense.

Like a beast your indulgences, and
pillows sank comfortably
in a kind of clause without a cause
without uttering a sound.

While flasks of wine and habitual traps
winked at such virginity
and now she fumbles in the backfield
humbling her hands.

LA NOTTE ERA una splendida canna di giunco
i suoi provvisori accecamenti erano di giunco
i suoi averi scappavano dalle mie mani
le sue filantropie anche erano di giunco.
Oh potessi avere la leggerezza della prosa
o di quel inverno che fu così ben racchiuso
fra i tetti impiantati: questa strada d'inverno
è come se qualcuno l'avesse saccheggiata.
Oh potessi realizzare la rissa degli angioli
indovinati fra le colonne vertebrate, così
come la strada precipita senza segno, senso
per un vuoto putiferio per un mistico
soliloquio.

THE NIGHT WAS a splendid reed
its temporary blinding was of reed
its belongings slipped from my hands
its philanthropies were also of reed.
Oh to have the lightness of prose
or of that winter so well contained
between the implanted roofs: this winter road
appears as if someone had looted it.
Oh to realize the angels' brawl
fathomed among the vertebrate columns, the way
the road plummets without sign, sense
of an empty uproar of a mystic
soliloquy.

a Shubert

Una melodia colore arancione aveva suonato
nelle mie orecchie così attente al solfeggio
d'un violino abbastanza netto da toccarmi
perfino quelle mie fibre nervose (il
gran cuore) che mi tiravano per i capelli
mentre danzavo con la melanconia quella
sera che non ci fu posta.

Melodia eterna e inesplosa, melodia
di sentimenti che non possono violarsi
nel segreto tombale dell'apostolo: apostolo
di cosa? – d'una quasi disperata a volte
allegra, esposizione dei vostri quadri
mentali, sentimentali e ordinari: l'amore
in una scatola ben chiusa non ebbe tempo
di chiedere scusa.

to Shubert

An orange melody had sounded
in my ears so attentive to the solfeggio
of a violin keen enough to touch
even the fibers of my nerves (the
big heart) pulling me by the hair
while I was dancing with melancholy that
evening when there was no post.

Eternal and unexploded melody, melody
of feelings that can't be violated
in the dead secret of the apostle—apostle
of what?—of an almost desperate sometimes
blithe, exposition of your mental,
sentimental and nondescript pictures: love
in a locked box had no time
to apologize.

INNESTO NEL VIVERE
la tua colpa (un
pedinaggio)
non mi feci avanti coi miei fiori, perché
tu eri ancora meditabondo
il cuore
curvo per eccellenza nella sua dimora
guardando se qualche verità inedita
ancora potesse provocarmi.

La piazza come una vecchia tristezza
alle due di notte deserta era e distante
parasentimenti
cerchi contusi (l'inutile
ronda)
nel senso guardingo della parola ti
credesti libera per un istante.

I GRAFT INTO living
your guilt
(tailing)
I didn't come forward with my flowers, because
you were still brooding
the heart
arched par excellence in its dwelling
checking to see if some new truth
could still provoke me.

The square like an old sadness
at two in the morning was deserted and distant,
parasentiments
injured circles (the useless
patrol)
in the wary sense of the word you
believed yourself free for an instant.

QUESTO TROVARE LA via al tuo cuore
che divorando preparai da buongustaio
la luna tolta di mezzo
con lunghe gambe promiscue (una responsabilità
scettica). Far tacere
la luna con la sua faccia promiscua,
una miseria forse ma che
comunque riempisse il vuoto della campana
di vetro blu.

Blu nel vetro, una persona che pensa
avere tenuto duro dieci giorni contando
con le mani che oramai annaspavano
l'alluminio scomparendo dai
tetti d'auto
reperibilità del tempo perduto vaticinando
quel tuo presente tutto irreperibile,
uncinando il grottesco gesto della
confessione.

THIS FINDING THE way to your heart
that devouring I'd prepared as a gourmet
removing the moon
with long promiscuous legs (a skeptical
responsibility). Silence
the moon with its promiscuous face,
a pittance perhaps but that
nonetheless could fill the void
of the blue glass bell.

Blue in the glass, a person who thinks
they held on for ten days counting
on their hands that by now fumbled
the aluminum disappearing from
the roofs of cars
availability of time past, prophesizing
your present wholly unavailable,
hooking the grotesque gesture of the
confession.

SOLO I FATTI, reprimere i sentimenti
poi ritrovi una «persona» che s'aggancia
fortemente al pavimento, i bricconi
le piccole vie pannellate, le testate
anche i grandi riverberi della tua immaginazione.

Piccoli neri su corona di fil di ferro
fatti concordano, espongono, giustificando
ed altri (che poi divennero te) quel
obliterare ogni passo della tua vita
sentimentale.

Furono una corona? La portasti espellendo
fiori mescolati all'avena? Rimanendo
un logico bastonarsi quel correre dei
tempi fu come una grafia utile, desiderabile
necessaria.

Rivale al cuore alle passioni (molto
usate e celebrate) desti filo da torcere
a quel nesso giuridico che operava nella
tua testa che forzatamente rubando al
ventre (ombra delle tue pupille) un

rafforzarsi della ragione, salvò quel
che poté, nell'ombra ragionando d'amore
mentre in via di trapasso celebravi
la quinta edizione del tuo errore.

JUST THE FACTS, repressing your feelings
then you find a "person" hooked
securely to the floor, rascals
small paneled streets, headings
and the great reverberations of your imagination.

Small dots on a wire wreath
facts agree, expose, justifying
and others (who then became you) that
obliterating of every step of your love
life.

Were they a crown? Did you wear it by expelling
flowers mixed with oats? It remained
a logical bludgeoning that elapsing
of time like a useful, desirable
necessary script.

Rival of heart of passions (much
used and celebrated) you gave a hard time
to that legal knot functioning in
your head that forcibly stealing from the
womb (shadow of your pupils) a

strengthening of reason, saved what
it could, in the shadows talking of love
while mid-passing you celebrated
the fifth edition of your error.

LA VACCINAZIONE, QUEL mio scrivere
per non averti potuto parlare in faccia
fatalità irrompendo
con una barba di cinque settimane
mortificarmi attorno ad un punto morto.

Un verbo è come un altro o è usuale
non potendo reperire dal
tuo sorriso altro che l'irreparabile.

Che vi fosse un pasto intero ad attendermi
grigio però vero
mangiando calmi
la rinascita dei nervi
mentre con metafisiche intenzioni
ricercandoti per tetre strade
il gas che stingeva le mani le pareti
cercando nell'avvenire il presente
si presentarono senza tare
puntando magari ai semi distrutti nella mente
in punta di piedi vi scrissi.

VACCINATION, MY WRITING
given I couldn't speak to your face
fatality bursting
with a five-week beard
mortifying myself about a deadlock.

One verb is like another or it's common
not being able to retrieve from
your smile more than the irreparable.

May there be a whole meal waiting for me
gray but real
eating you soothe
the rebirth of your nerves
while with metaphysical intentions
looking for you on gloomy roads
the gas fading the hands the walls
searching the future for the present
they presented themselves as flawless
maybe tipping at seeds destroyed in the mind
on tiptoe I wrote to you.

ACCORGENDOSI DI ME si accorse d'essere
ancora vivo e *mezzo morto*; assieme a
noi a me a te quanti magazzini dietro
le porte!

Acque stagne rivoluzionano il mio cuore
ho aspettato tanto a lungo il tuo cuore
che fasto sarebbe serbarsi intatti per
una lunga cura indolore!

Un colore forse freddo e stanco insieme
insieme siamo piccoli e giganti insieme
il ricordo della tua presenza è sempre
una lusinga, un lungo indolore parto
per chi lo porta.

Ho scoperto il tuo colore stanco e freddo
ho rivissuto le notti migliori e il
freddo non fu mai così lontano dalla
mia porta, da farmi credere che eri
tu imbattibile.

Ma fra le fresche e dolci case s'abituano
mezzadri: i loro illustri predecessori
li hanno tutti abituati al tatto: al
duro silenzio.

Ai patti non so stare? Quale insicurezza
mi fece così pazza? Però sempre così
attenta alle tue parole?

Mezzo candelabro ci sviò: vi furono
fiori deposti su le tue tombe: ne crebbi

Noticing me he realized he was
still alive and half dead; together with
us with me with you how many storerooms
behind the doors!

Stagnant waters revolutionize my heart
I awaited your heart for so long
how splendid it would be to remain intact
for a long painless cure!

A color perhaps cold and tired together
together we are small and giant together
the memory of your presence is always
a flattery, a long painless birth
for those who bear it.

I discovered your cold and tired color
I relived the best nights and the
cold was never so far from
my door, to make me believe you
were impregnable.

But among the fresh and sweet homes sharecroppers
grow accustomed: their illustrious predecessors
have accustomed them all to touch: to the
stony silence.

Can't I keep a pact? What insecurity
made me so crazy? But always so
attentive to your words?

Half a candelabrum diverted us: there were
flowers placed on your tombs: I raised

uno: era indolore.

Lo scritto che in me è folle risponde
a tutto questo dolore con parole sempre
spero sempre vere.

E vero è il tuo linguaggio: vero il
nostro? Vero questo parto indolore? più
violento, più triste, più calmo, più
dolce d'una tua carezza in fronte.

Bifronte ho urgenza di conoscerti: son
doppia, son mal fatta, son incolore
quando manca la tua gioia esplosa una
mattina fresca e bianca.

one: it was painless.

The writing that's folly in me answers
to all this pain always with words
I hope always true.

And your language is true: is ours
true? True this painless birth? more
violent, sadder, calmer, sweeter
than you caressing my face.

Two-faced I'm impelled to meet you: I'm
double, I'm poorly made, I'm colorless
when your joy goes missing, exploding
one fresh and white morning.

VEDEVO NELL'ORA PIÙ oscura il tramonto
di gelide giornate, rivalutando questioni
che non mi appartenevano affatto. E
nel giro di pochi giorni queste diurne
dannazioni (ogni giorno uno spogliatoio)
s'applicavano a farmi stringere vanamente
una sequela di arrangiamenti, piccoli
boschi tramontati che avrei tanto voluto
fossero pace semplice.

Il canone della tua vita pratica è questa
furia di iniettare sangue in ferite
che non provocano disagio ma solo un
disarmarsi delle intenzioni; il non
averle e pur volerle.

Volendole ti accorgevi d'esserti tanto
frainteso!

IN THE DARKEST hour I saw the sunset
of frosty days, re-evaluating matters
that had nothing to do with me. And
in the space of a few days these daytime
damnations (each day an undressing)
applied themselves to make me strengthen in vain
a sequel of arrangements, small
sunset woods that I'd have liked so much
to be simple peace.

The canon of your practical life is this
frenzy of injecting blood into wounds
that don't cause discomfort but only
a disarming of intentions; not
having them yet still wanting them.

Wanting them you found you'd wholly
misunderstood yourself!

Compianto paradiso: pace in terra anche
se solo per un istante: non l'avrai!
mai: né puoi calcolarla, provocarla,
costruirla pezzo a pezzo.

Il male col suo bene rifà la strada
ogni giorno invernale e a te sembra
che debba non far altro che attenuarti
la condizione civile in cui vivi.

Nessuna gioia nasce, può partorire un
così fresco vento o sole da contraddire
la tua sagacità: ti distruggi un poco
per poi contare sull'orlo delle dita

quanta freschezza fu persa scappando.

LAMENTED PARADISE: PEACE on earth if
only for a moment: you won't have it!
ever: nor can you calculate it, provoke it,
build it piece by piece.

Evil with its good retraces its steps
every winter day and it seems to you
that it should do nothing but mitigate
the civil status you live in.

No joy is born, can give birth to such
a cool wind or sun to contradict
your sagacity: you destroy yourself a little
then count on the brink of your fingers

how much freshness was lost in the escape.

Ho visto il cielo gongolarsi: era purpureo
poi mano a mano si schiariva ed io mi
schiarivo con esso: non riuscivo ad
essere esso!

Quando fu grigio a chiaro non fu più
cielo: ah un attimo sfuggente che perfino
io distrussi!

Quando il cielo tornò ad essere quella
macchina sguaiata dei nostri inverni
cittadini dimenticai quasi che potesse
essere all'alba un fulgore.

A tradimento il blu si fece incolore
la profondità dell'alba e della notte
sfumò in agonia di primo mattino.

I saw the sky gloat: it was purple
then gradually cleared and I
cleared with it: I couldn't
be it!

When it went from gray to light it was no longer
sky: ah a fleeting moment even this
I destroyed!

When the sky went back to being that
coarse engine of our city
winters I almost forgot that it could
be a blaze at dawn.

Without warning the blue turned colorless
the depth of dawn and night
faded into agony at daybreak.

SE MAI NELLA mia mente disperazione
ebbe luogo: se mai nel mio cuore dubbio
ebbe posto: se mai nei miei piedi forza
urtò: se mai nella mia lacerata mente
si curvò l'uragano.

Se mai nel mio piede ebbe posto la violenza
era per sottrarmi agli altri che preparai
lo stambugio: se mai vi fu una violenza
era per prepararmi agli altri.

Se mai nella mia mente nacque il desiderio
d'essere io stessa vittima e carnefice
se mai nel mio cuore obbediva il carme

della desta porta alla speranza.

IF EVER IN my mind despair
took root: if ever in my heart doubt
took root: if ever in my feet force
struck: if ever in my torn mind
the hurricane curled.

If ever in my foot violence took root
it was to dodge the others that I prepared
this hovel: if ever there was violence
it was to prepare myself for the others.

If ever in my mind was born a desire
to be both victim and slayer
if ever in my heart the ode

of the lithe door brought hope.

FIGLIA DI UN amore che ti divorò fui
mai quella che scelse? O che travolse
in un gaudio completo? La libertà di
ricevere e di dare è dei pochi – altri
combattono delusi, con se stessi e la
loro verginità combattuta, imbattuta.

Stanziare riserve contro i contadini
è tale urgenza da possedere anche i
migliori, che si sono costruiti con
le mani nel sangue, non visti, non scoperti
e la comprensione degli altri è poca
visione, se ricordiamo il frastagliato
amore che ci legò alla giustizia.

È la giustizia un caso di coscienza?
È l'amore un possedere troppo voracemente?
Nelle notti che passano come bianchi
lenzuoli vi è un'urgenza che ci divora
malgrado le molte premesse ad una vita
intieramente dedicata alla ragione.

DAUGHTER OF A devouring love did I
ever get to choose? Or to sweep away
in complete joy? Freedom of
receiving and giving is for the few—others
fight on, disappointed in themselves and
their virginity, embattled, unbroken.

Allocating reserves against the peasants
it's urgent enough to possess even the
best, who built themselves with their
bloodied hands, unseen, undiscovered
and the understanding of others is scant
vision, if we remember the jagged
love that tied us to justice.

Is justice a case of conscience?
Does love possess too voraciously?
In the nights passing like white
sheets there's an urgency devouring us
despite the many premises of a life
dedicated entirely to reason.

CONCATENAZIONE DI CAUSE: hai visto l'ombra
aggirarsi per foreste chiuse, e solo
all'alba del tramonto ti si offrì un
volto in petto riconosciuto per tuo
fratello che allungava la tua corta,
pericolante esistenza.

Ebbi timore di offendere la mano tesa
offesa: ebbi timore della mia pace troppo
solitaria.

Chiudendo il verso ho intravisto una
libertà che non perdura: hai fiato troppo
grosso tu con le tue lacrime gettate
ai piedi del primo venuto.

Bombe lacrimogene: hanno scelto un campo
a te del tutto indifferente per fraternizzare
con lo sciopero della rinuncia a
te stesso: che eri tu, per cui il mio

batticuore non vuole pace ma solo oblio

nel ramo più elevato del cielo.

CONCATENATION OF CAUSES: you've seen the shadow
wandering through closed forests, and only
as sunset dawned a face was offered
recognized in your breast as your
brother who extended your short,
precarious existence.

I was fearful of offending the offered
offended hand: I feared my too solitary
peace.

Closing the verse I glimpsed a
freedom that doesn't last: you're almost
out of breath you with your tears cast
at the feet of the first comer.

Teargas bombs: they chose a field
completely indifferent to you to fraternize
with the strike of renouncing
yourself: that it was you, and so my

beating heart doesn't want peace only oblivion

on the highest branch of the sky.

QUANTI CAMPI CHE come spugna vorrebbero
arricchire il tuo passato, anche il tuo
presente soffocato.

Quante viuzze del tutto pittoresche
che tu vorresti tramutare in significato
dell'essenza di questa tua sofferenza.

Ma geme nell'essenza della tua sofferenza
un desiderio di sonno o di carne. Oh

come i merli taciono! Hanno confuso
la tua idea della pace con il tramonto

che offrì ai tuoi occhi penduli solo
un sofisticato sequestro della tua brama
d'essere solo, e te stesso.

How many fields sponge-like would hope
to enrich your past, even your
suffocated present.

How many utterly picturesque alleys
that you'd like to mold into the sense

of the essence of this sufferance of yours.

But it moans in the essence of your sufferance
a desire for sleep or meat. Oh

how silent the blackbirds! They mistook
your idea of peace for the sunset

that offered your pendulous eyes only
a sophisticated confiscation of your yearning
to be alone, and yourself.

QUANTI RAMI HANNO gli oliveti che tu
vedi solo come carta vetrata! Il palcoscenico
preme per sostituire la tua bellezza
al volo obliquo, distrutto, del tuo
amore e della tua scoraggiata rinuncia

a quel che offriva il dono della solitudine
terrorizzata, terrorizzante, che premeva
rompendo gli scaffali, e quell'intruglio

che ti querelava. Questi campi ottusi
nel tuo fieno!

Hai avvelenato la tua esistenza cercando
il conforto della prosa mentre poesia
ricercava la tua gloria.

How many branches have the olive groves
that you see simply as sandpaper! The stage
presses to replace your beauty
with oblique flight, destroyed, of your
love and your discouraged renunciation

of what offered the gift of terrified
terrifying solitude, pressing
breaking shelves, and that concoction

suing you. These obtuse fields
in your hay!

You've poisoned your existence seeking
the solace of prose while poetry
sought your glory.

SEI NEL MIO petto, ma poi ti ritrovo,
ma poi ti perdo, ma poi sei lì, e non
vuoi addomesticare il mio sangue che
non ha altra urgenza che di chinarsi
sul tuo tutto indifferente corpo che
annega mentre m'infilo nel letto.

Sei nel mio petto o là ti ritrovo quando
non vedo nel campo o nella miniera altro
che sigarette mezze spente che rinunciano
al significare.

Significando in questo accoppiarsi del
tutto immaginario la tua unione brancolante
in un sospiro di sollievo, ché nel mio
petto brilli avventuroso, trovai una

sorta di pace mal costruita mentre battezzavano
le pecore nell'ovile.

You're in my breast, but then I find you,
but then I lose you, but then there you are, and you
don't want to tame my blood that
knows no need other than bending down
on your all-indifferent body
drowning while I slip into bed.

You're in my breast or I find you there when
I don't see in the field or the mine anything
other than half-smoked cigarettes renouncing
their meaning.

Meaning in this wholly imaginary
coupling your fumbling union
with a sigh of relief, shining adventurously in
my breast, I found a

poorly built sort of peace while they baptized
the sheep in the fold.

PERDONA LE COLPE come io rimetto i terrori
abroga le dure feste, i fasti, i languori
festa della tua carne, le
sonore gioie.

Con la punta della lingua sbiadita
versi trasparenti
una libidine di saggezza.

Ho vinto solo il vizio
di strapparmi la fede
a contatto con il mio regno di improvvise
somministrazioni di dubbi
il mio senso di continuità a singhiozzo.

Forgive our faults as I forgive the terrors
abrogate the harsh feasts, the fanfares, the languor
feast of your flesh, the
resonant joys.

With the tip of a faded tongue
transparent verses
a lust for wisdom.

I won only the vice
to tear away my faith
in touch with my kingdom of sudden
administration of doubts
my sense of continuity in fits and starts.

E VELENO FORZARSI per nervi occulti
fino a rimaneggiare le vie occulte
mentre l'affanno consideravo indubbio
gli affetti sospiravano senilmente
nell'impianto d'una civiltà costruita
sul rimpianto.

Il balbettare
grandi frasi
la luna come un pezzo di carta straccia
fertili visite alle donne
mentre con le mammelle incrostate
verdi stanze analfabete coprivano invariabili
finestre.

AND POISON STRAINING through occult nerves
to the point of reshuffling occult paths
while I considered the anxiety indubitable
affections sighed senile at the
founding of a civilization built
on the forlorn.

Stuttering
big sentences
the moon like a piece of wastepaper
fertile visits to women
while with encrusted tits
green illiterate stanzas covered invariable
windows.

LA SEVERA VITA dei giustiziati rinnovava
la scoperta d'un abisso che era e non
era il loro disinteresse ma una cosa
ben più sicura: la loro costanza, la
loro incostanza, il loro regime feudale
e le cagnotte tenute al laccio. La costanza
di questa loro interessata fedeltà che
era fedeltà tout court, quella loro
fedeltà a speranze perché venissero
deluse, quel loro sperare! così tragici
nell'immedesimarsi nella tragica farsa.

Un gioco o un altro, una carestia o
un'altra, un gioco di circostanze o
un altro, una fama mondiale o un dovere
obbedito – il resto è da cancellarsi
sì che il resto non appaia più fra le
liste degli annegati, i perseguitati
i rimpianti e le loro doleanze.

Cara vita che mi sei andata perduta
con te avrei fatto faville se solo tu
non fosti andata perduta.

THE HARD LIFE of the executed renovated
the discovery of an abyss that was and was
not their disinterest but something
much more secure: their constancy, their
inconstancy, their feudal regime
and leashed flunkies. Constancy
of their interested fealty that
was fealty tout court, that
fealty to hope so they'd be
disappointed, in their hoping! so tragic
in their identification with the tragic farce.

One game or another, one famine or
another, one game of circumstance or
another, one worldly fame or a duty
obeyed—the rest to be canceled
so the rest no longer appears on the
lists of the drowned, the persecuted
the forlorn and their *doléance*.

Dear life that was lost to me
with you I'd have sparkled if only you
hadn't been lost to me.

ININTERROTTA LA MANO guida ancóra impotenza
nelle sue carni lentigginose così piene

di sale della terra che mai mostrò ad
altri altro che oreficerie, colombi,
rivolte o massacri.

Contaminata la gioia da parenti illustri
un dovere in più illustra situazioni
che non vengono chiarite: sei tu! a
non chiarirle: donna ed amore, forza
o poliziotto: guerra o revisione tutti
sistemati in un intero mondo verde di
lusinghe al povero e all'imbarazzato
che non potendo pane ai denti e al cuore
portare illustra sgabellando la sua
intera moralità.

Hand uninterrupted still guides impotence
in its freckled flesh so full

of salt of the earth that never showed to
others other than goldsmiths, pigeons,
riots or massacres.

Joy contaminated by illustrious relatives
an extra duty illustrates unclarified
situations: it's you! who
won't clarify them: woman and love, force
or officer: war or revision all
settled in a whole green world of
flattery of the poor and embarrassed
who unable to bring bread to their lips
and hearts illustrate their whole morality
by paying duty.

CERCHI UNA GIUSTIZIA: non l'avrai mai
ma il tuo cuore che in così largo dono
donò suoi figli (le viti arrampicanti)
osa, non osa, vuole, non vuole, è destinato
ad essere proprio come tutti gli altri?

Cerchi una risposta con impazienza e
scrivi versi così facendo di un caso
quasi pietoso (lo chiamarono illustre
poi) una più vasta larga conoscenza

di ogni tuo movente.

You look for justice: you'll never find it
but your heart that with such a large gift
gifted its children (climbing vines)
dares, doesn't, wants, doesn't, is meant
to be just like everyone else?

You look impatiently for an answer and
write verse thus making of an almost
sad case (they called it illustrious
then) a vast and broader understanding

of your every motive.

QUALE AZIONE SCEGLIERE, prevedere, ereditare?
Un pezzo di pane a cane senza museruola
è meglio di questo scrivere in bianchi
versi di getti lagrimogeni, a branchi
di gente tutta senza importanza o museruola

che scrive vincendo e perdendo tutte
le cause: mentre fuori il tempo gode
e esplode, senza la tua intima perplessità
intimità di cose andate e perdute mentre
tutt'occupata a scrivere versi bianchi
andavi leggendo quel che non si poté

fare.

WHAT ACTION TO choose, predict, inherit?
A lump of dough to an unmuzzled dog
it's better than this writing in blank
verse of teargas jets, to herds
of people all without importance or muzzles

who write by winning and losing every
cause: while outside time enjoys
and explodes, without your intimate perplexity
intimacy of things long gone while
busy writing blank verse
you'd read what couldn't

be done.

FINCHÉ NON DIVENTA vanità non è libertà
ma è solo l'anima in pena che si descrive
mentre paradossalmente non si prescrive
altro che accomodamenti.

Perché così solitaria: è per esempio:
questo che ti lega al foglio di carta
e alla bianca pagina (si cancellò poi)
e in ciò facendo tu vedesti aprirsi
altre scarse ragioni di fare il morto.

Morto o vivo che crudeltà: non hai alcun
modo d'esprimere buone intenzioni che
hanno tutta l'apparenza agli occhi incuriositi
d'esser tutt'altro che libertà.

Faccende oscure ti riempiono la mente
di torture mal e difficili da sopportare
ma tu nella tua chiarezza impervertita
vedrai un giorno forse, forse (e ne
sono sicura quasi) (se non muori) pervertirsi
la tua anima in un più generoso dono

che è lo scrivere adorando e perdendo
ogni giorno della tua giornata perdendo
la facilità che tu hai a descrivere
queste minuzie di così poca importanza.

As long as it doesn't become vanity it's not liberty
for it's only the lost soul describing itself
while paradoxically not prescribing itself
other than accommodation.

Why so solitary: for example:
what ties you to the sheet of paper
and to the blank page (then deleted)
and in so doing you saw revealed
a few other reasons to pretend to be dead.

Dead or alive what cruelty: you've no
way of expressing good intentions that
give to curious eyes the appearance
of being anything but liberty.

Dark matters fill your mind
with torture hard to bear
but you in your unperverted clarity
one day you'll see perhaps, perhaps (and
I'm almost sure) (if you don't die) your soul
perverting itself with a more generous gift

which is writing by worshiping and losing
every day of your day losing
the ease you have in describing
these minutiae of such little importance.

MOLLE RIVERBERO DEL cuscino fatto per
riposare e dormire senza tregua quando
con il lunario semispento accettavi
una sigaretta e ne accendevi un'altra.

Dopo, dopo molte notti avevi visto ancora
lampeggiare quel fuoco d'accendigas
che ti scopriva la fronte e i seni di
solito nascosti.

Luna semipiena ostenta tu questa ricchezza
io non vedo altro che povertà in questo
mangiar lumache nella grandezza d'una
biblica arretratezza.

SOFT REVERBERATION OF the pillow made for
unbroken rest and sleep when
with the moonshine half-spent you accepted
a cigarette and lit another.

Later, after many nights you'd seen
that gas lighter blinking again
uncovering your forehead and breasts
usually hidden.

Half-full moon be the one to flaunt this wealth
I see nothing but poverty in this
eating of snails in the greatness of a
biblical backwater.

PSICOLOGICAMENTE ADEMPIENTE è il diamante
mia fortezza mio colore mia pronuncia
variante tra l'infanzia e la prostituzione
caffèlatte per i prostrati.

La verità non si lasciava differenziare
occhio di bue che ti guarda mangiando
i suoi trionfi sempre una agiacenza
ad un avvenire che distruggevi distratta.

La tristezza è come un urlo di sirena
chiamami le industriali sentenze del fato
ma rimani al di là delle mie terre furiose
carne che ti spandi splendida per poi risuscitare.

Pioggia miserissima stingendo nel fracasso
delle passioni anche il tuo rosso occhio;
una violenza carnale s'aggirava per le mandibole
asciutte dello sguardo, quando l'innocenza

stremata di piaceri, s'assise sull'erba umida.

Psychologically dexterous the diamond
is my fortress my color my pronunciation
varying between childhood and prostitution
caffè latte for the prostrate.

Truth couldn't be differentiated
bull's eye that looks at you eating
its triumphs always adjacent
to a future that, distracted, you destroyed.

Sadness is like a siren scream
call for me the industrial sentences of fate
but stay beyond my furious lands
flesh splendidly spreading then rising again.

Most miserable rain waning in the uproar
of passions also your red eye;
a carnal violence lurked around the gaze's
dry jaws, when innocence

worn out from pleasures, sat on the damp grass.

L'AMORE CHE CI divide e ci unisce subisce
incartamenti, spezie e riunioni di partito
combattuto da istorie di partito affatto
trascurabili mentre m'addormentavo sul
tovagliolo.

Infatti i dati dettero ragione alla
promiscua cella nella ragione che ci
forzò a separarci ad ammazzarci mentre
covavano gli astri i loro sogni di una
distante patria nell'ignoto.

Quale qualunquismo in questi tuoi versi
decapitati da forze ignote rivoltate
al cielo con le sue visioni che trovandosi
di fronte a lotte superiori non rinunciò
a vivere mentre incassava.

LOVE THAT DIVIDES us and unites us endures
dossiers, spices and party meetings
fought by party stories completely
negligible while I fell asleep on the
napkin.

In fact data proved correct the
promiscuous cell as the reason
forcing us to separate to kill one another while
the stars were harboring their dreams of a
distant homeland in the unknown.

What indifference in your verses
beheaded by unknown forces turned
to the sky with its visions that finding itself
confronted with higher struggles didn't give up
living while taking it in.

PRONTEZZA DI RIFLESSI: sàlvati se puoi
gridò il naufrago che tanto contava
sulla permissibilità degli incontri
che fortuitamente sembrando abbastanza
decorosi sembrarono poi indecorosi.

Sàlvati se puoi: hai una arringa per
difesa: l'acciuga che tu tenesti stretta
fra le braccia che si muovevano muovendo
l'aria.

Fingi d'essere un benpensante: semmai
sarai solitamente versata ad ingegnarti
più del solito.

Fingi di amare: o ami davvero con una
disperazione o ribellione che non è
proprio nel tuo carattere.

Di chi la colpa: di questo pulcino che
nascondendosi dietro due parafrasi saltò
piedi in aria cercando un obolo, una
maniera di sopravvivere.

Non ve n'è: soltanto uno smercio di
giocattoli!

Quick reflexes: save yourself
shouted the castaway who counted heavily
on the permissibility of the encounters
that fortuitously seeming decorous
enough seemed then indecorous.

Save yourself: you have a harangue for
defense: the anchovy you held tight
in your moving arms moving
the air.

You pretend to be a conformist: if anything
you'll be able to figure it out as ever
better than ever.

You pretend to love: or you truly love with a
despair or rebellion that isn't
really in your character.

Who's to blame for this: for this hatchling who
hiding behind two paraphrases jumped
feet in the air seeking an offering, a
way to survive.

There is none: only toys
marked down!

AMORE BLU E verde: che collasso mi
prese quel giorno che tu blu e verde
sei rinverdito con il motoscafo. Quel
motoscafo giallognolo con le sue rime
traverse che cotonano la tua traversata
piangendo nel retro.

Quale fiore da cogliere! quale sincope
da barattare con il dolore del tuo
sangue!

Verde brutta linea a rovescio sembri
mia pura cristallina sorgente una brutta
esperienza.

Love blue and green: what a breakdown I
had that day when blue and green you
greened with your motorboat. That
yellowish motorboat with its crosswise
rhymes combing your crossing
crying in the back.

Which flower to pick! which syncope
to trade for the pain of your
blood!

Ugly green backhanded line you seem
my pure crystalline source an ugly
experience.

Mentre mi avvicinai alle pareti odoravano
anche di sangue queste pareti che invece
sudavano.

Notti fà ho visto sperdersi ardori che
punendosi e pulendosi si dimostrarono
incapaci di anelare verso l'infinito.

Ma mare e giostra hanno ugual ardore
vi fu un caldo precipuo amore – precipitoso
nel garantirsi agli altri.

A se stessi finsero bombe aperte e a
mano dire: notte tempo ho rivaleggiato
con l'ardore!

A se stessi finsero bombe a mano dire
notte tempo ho rivaleggiato con l'ardore
e non mi sommuove rissa alcuna.

A se stessi finsero di dire amore ardore
a se stessi dissero perso l'amore che
tanta battaglia dette a l'odore di questa

condiscendente rivalità.

As I approached the walls also odorous
with blood these walls that instead
were sweating.

Nights ago I saw ardor go astray
punishing and preening it proved itself
incapable of striving toward the infinite.

But sea and carousel have equal ardor
there was a warm primary amour—precipitous
in ensuring itself to others.

They feigned bombs and
grenades to say: nighttime I rivaled
ardor!

They feigned grenades to say
nighttime I rivaled ardor
and I'm not shaken by any brawl.

They feigned to say amour ardor
they told themselves lost is the amour that
so fiercely battled the odor of this

condescending rivalry.

UN ORRORE DI bombe che cadono tremanti
voracemente impegnate a sostituirti
il pane, oh sommossa contadina che vai
cercando invece il brodo, il buono brodo.

Vittoria armata sino ai denti e una
sinistra causa appariscono povere al
contrasto che si fece tra due banditi
e le loro circostanze.

Tubi rosa, rosi dalla pioggia che indaffarata
scuote le vigorie del mondo.

A HORROR OF shivering falling bombs
voraciously committed to replacing
bread for you, oh peasant revolt looking
instead for the broth, the good broth.

Victory armed to the teeth and a
sinister cause appear impoverished
in the contrast drawn between two bandits
and their circumstances.

Rosy tubes, eroded by the busy rain
shaking the vigor of the world.

NELLE CENE DISTILLATE
l'ombra si grattava la pancia
astratta.

L'idea
di un libro mi venne in mente per sbaglio
scegliendo per amministrare questi miei
beni una scena vuota.

Vi fu invece una
iterazione,
interurbana coraggiosa:
nelle ore inferme del mattino.

At the distilled dinners
the shadow scratched its abstract
belly.

The idea
for a book came to me by accident
choosing to administer these goods
of mine an empty scene.

Instead there was an
iteration,
brave long-distance call:
in the sickly morning hours.

I FIORI VENGONO in dono e poi si dilatano
una sorveglianza acuta li silenzia
non stancarsi mai dei doni.

Il mondo è un dente strappato
non chiedetemi perché
io oggi abbia tanti anni
la pioggia è sterile.

Puntando ai semi distrutti
eri l'unione appassita che cercavo
rubare il cuore d'un altro per poi servirsene.

La speranza è un danno forse definitivo
le monete risuonano crude nel marmo
della mano.

Convincevo il mostro ad appartarsi
nelle stanze pulite d'un albergo immaginario
v'erano nei boschi piccole vipere imbalsamate.

Mi truccai a prete della poesia
ma ero morta alla vita
le viscere che si perdono
in un tafferuglio
ne muori spazzato via dalla scienza.

Il mondo è sottile e piano:
pochi elefanti vi girano, ottusi.

FLOWERS ARRIVE AS a gift and then dilate
a keen surveillance silences them
never get tired of gifts.

The world is a pulled tooth
don't ask me why
today I'm ancient
the rain is sterile.

Aiming for destroyed seeds
you were the withered union I sought
stealing someone's heart to then make use of it.

Hope may be a definitive wrong
coins harshly resound in the marble
of the hand.

I convinced the monster to withdraw
to the clean rooms of an imaginary hotel
in the woods there were small embalmed vipers.

I dressed as a priest of poetry
but I was dead to life
viscera getting lost
in a scuffle
you die swept up by science.

The world is subtle and flat:
few elephants roam it, obtusely.

PROVENIENZA DI *CAOTCHUC*
scorgo un ritratto
che era il mio sul muro pannellato, le
piccole rose (masturbati disegni)
la parete che nella giallastra luce serale
pareva sbiadire il mio corpo.

Organi dei sensi che nella mente tramutano
impigliano la memoria di frasi
pullulendo questi ormoni, questa
faccia di lividi.

Vuoto meschino, ingoiare quel rospo
spaziature convincenti
caverna
dei dentifrici, spalla fredda lancinata
caso, freccia o lungomare
ch'io non vedo essendo seduta.

Puntando folli occhi riserbati alle
vostre giunture di cera
che essendo
bambole di cera non hanno occhi.

Cristo insonne stendesse abitudini...
oh cuore trafelato
dalle larghe falde tue castane oh povero
cuore doveroso.

Oh povero cuore polveroso!

Provenance of *caoutchouc*
I see a portrait
that was mine on the paneled wall, the
small roses (masturbated drawings)
the wall appearing to whiten my body
in the yellowish evening light.

Sense organs transmuting in the mind
entangling memory of sentences
these hormones swarming, this
face of bruises.

Petty void, swallowing that pill
convincing spacing
cave
of toothpaste, cold stabbing shoulder,
case, arrow or waterfront
I can't see being seated.

Crazed staring eyes reserved for
your wax joints
given that
wax dolls have no eyes.

Sleepless Christ spread habits…
oh breathless heart
with your broad brown flaps oh poor
dutiful heart.

Oh poor dusty heart!

IL SOLE A scatti ci risveglia dal lungo
inverno della mente che intestardita
o impazzita credeva trovare luce solo
in se stessa; ma oggi ha gonfie vele
questo sole e la mente non può rifiutare
l'immonda ingiustizia del sole che a
sprazzi colora la pelle di paure inacidite.

Un sole, una merce, una luce che violenta
il cuore farraginoso impacchettato
di violente crisi.

Coinvolto in una lussuria di abeti egli
fracassa ogni lunga attesa e si rivolge
alla lunga danza che ravvolge le sue
ramificazioni; quanti onori! e quante

perdite! sciovinista il cuore si domanda
perché in così buia cava egli riposa,
quali furono i suoi errori a condurlo
in così strana causa.

Una causa errata? mistero più vorace
non ci fu data la misericordia che produce
le tristi inabilità.

Twitchy sun awakens us from the long
winter of the mind that stubborn
or crazed believed light was found only
in itself; but today this sun's sails are
full and the mind can't refuse
the filthy injustice of the sun that off
and on colors the skin of sour fears.

A sun, a commodity, a light that violates
the farraginous heart wrapped up
in violent crisis.

Involved in a lusting of fir trees it
smashes every long wait and turns
to the long dance enveloping its
ramifications; so many honors! so many

losses! the chauvinist heart wonders
why it rests in such a dark quarry,
what were its mistakes leading it
to such a strange cause.

A mistaken cause? most voracious mystery
we weren't shown mercy breeding
sad disabilities.

CON LA TERRA che sembra tremare di coincidenze
non ho fiato per gridare la mia indifferenza

WITH EARTH SEEMING to tremble from coincidences
I lack breath to shout my indifference

UN BLU CHE non è nemmeno blu o comunque
è un blu chiaro chiaro chiaro e la polvere
sembra mischiata all'aria essendo un
poco gialligno il cielo che è stesura
di sabbia.

Le case sono muri che come una lavagna
si cancellano, hanno anch'essi aria di
sabbia.

Ma la sabbia non ha voce e tristemente
rovina il paesaggio perché non può lei
stessa volare al cielo, votare quel suo

esistere!

A BLUE THAT'S not even blue or anyway
it's a light light light blue and dust
seems mixed with the air the sky being
a bit yellowish, a draft
of sand.

Houses are walls that like a blackboard
erase themselves, they also resemble
sand.

But sand has no voice and sadly
ruins the landscape because it can't
by itself veer to the sky, voting its

existence!

FILI PROGRAMMATI SI stirano tra albero
e albero: spezzarli, riuscire a non
essere forzati a mentirsi!

Ed era un'ora ancora che rimaneva
che rimanesse a noi, nel nostro non
volere partecipare a così scabra storia.

Crisi di crisantemi avvinse l'alloro,
vile si fece l'impero o dominio dell'amore:
era notte tarda, e già si vedevano

le prime stelle.

PRESET WIRES STRETCH from tree
to tree: break them, succeed at
not being forced to lie to oneself!

And it was an encore hour remaining
that remained to us, in our not
wanting to participate in such a crude tale.

Chrysanthemum crisis enticed the laurel,
vile became the domain or empire of love:
it was late at night, and one could already see

the first stars.

QUANTE STELLE FITTE e orgiastiche che
si riuniscono per combattere questa
melanconia ed il terrore che così facilmente
afferra chi non può dormire di notte
facilmente ingannato dalla marcia della
vita. Quanto ardore e poco ardore viene
somministrato da forze d'ordine mentre
invece tutto cade in deliquio.

E il deliquio è ardore e l'ardore è
misericordia e la misericordia non è
altro che ardore disfattosi con il vivere
disingannati.

Disinganno dopo ore di trambusto alleggerito
da una forza interna che preme per essere
finalmente quella che avrebbe potuto
essere prima che il mare d'inganno la
traesse a sé.

Ed è con inganno ed è con dolcezza ed
è con forza ed è con lacrime che ogni
forza svaporò nel volere essere come
altri che non si pavoneggiano: ma ad
ogni giro della strada sorgevano novelle

volontà di vivere fuori del tracciato
operato dalla nostra mente irrequieta,
e le conquiste così operate non sembravano
porre fine allo sgomento.

Uno sgomento totale, che non illumina
quelle quattro stagioni che monotonamente

How many dense and orgiastic stars
come together to fight this
melancholy and the terror that so easily
grips those who can't sleep at night
easily deceived by the march of
life. How much ardor and little ardor is
administered by law and order while
instead everything swoons.

And swoon is ardor and ardor is
mercy and mercy is nothing else
but ardor undone by disenchanted
living.

Disenchanted after hours of bustle eased
by an internal force pressing to be
finally the one that could have
been before the sea of deception
brought it to itself.

And it's with deception and sweetness and
it's with force and tears that every
force evaporated in wanting to be like
others who don't flaunt themselves: but at
every turn of the road a new willingness

to live off the beaten path arose
from our restless minds,
and conquests thus made didn't appear
to put an end to dismay.

A complete dismay, which doesn't illuminate
those four seasons monotonously

conquistano al loro ritmo l'uomo stanco
di combattere con se stesso e le delusioni

i suoi ritmi assediati dal torpore delle
sue vicende assortite nel bene e nel
male che finse di capire il perché di
tanta cruenta ingenuità, nel partire
per i boschi vivi, neri, tragici e vita
ancora lo trae a sé.

conquering at their own pace the man tired
of fighting with himself and his disappointments

his rhythms besieged by the torpor of
his assorted doings for better or for
worse who feigned to understand why
so much bloody naivete, in leaving
for the living woods, black, tragic and life
still draws him.

Dialogo con i Morti

scendete voi, abbracciate questa vostra
figlia che annaspa tra tomboloni e
mussulmani che giocano con le sue braccia
che invece, bianche, vorrebbero abbracciare
o strozzare ma mai fallire questi colpi
che diurnamente ricevono, pieni di
lividi e lividamente promuovete una
sete di dolcezza e aspra giustizia
oppure non lasciate più ch'io tormenti
(ed essi mi tormentano) questa mente
che muore ad ogni istante piena di
stretti nodi che ingombrano la sua
piana marcia ad un paese più bello introvabile
mentre muore lividamente anche la voglia
di essere più belli di quello che si
è.

Scendete, e scendete ancóra – e infilate
nella vostra banale gioia il significare
d'una vita che ballonzola rattristata
dalla piena potenza del male degli
altri e del mio – il non sapere difendermi
da ottusa voglia.

Vivere un istante o mezz'ora e poi
ritrovarsi per una svista del pensiero
ancora più ingombra di inessenziali
rabbie!

Voce in capitolo non ebbero le sagge

Dialogue with the Dead

descend, embrace your daughter
floundering among tumbles and
muslims playing with her arms
which, white, they'd like instead to embrace
or choke but never fail these blows
they daily receive, full of
bruises and bruised you promote a
thirst for sweetness and bitter justice
or you don't let me torment anymore
(and they torment me) this mind
dying at every instant full of
tight knots cluttering its level march
toward a more beautiful unattainable country
not to be found while, bruised, also dies the desire
to be more beautiful than one
is.

Descend, again and again—and slip
into your banal joy the meaning
of a life bouncing saddened
by the full power of others' evil
and of my own—not knowing how to defend myself
from obtuse desire.

Living an instant or half an hour and then
finding oneself due to an oversight
even more cluttered with inessential
angers!

The wise hands had no say in

mani: vi incontrai per poi farmi ostinatamente
massacrare da voi.

E il massacro volge in lussuria: e
la lussuria in estasi contemplata nel
grano sifilitico che s'attorciglia al
mio collo, stremato dai troppi abbandoni.

Abbandonarsi al vuoto sesso e poi ritenersi
anche insudiciati dalla nera pece del
fare così angusto dei poveri.

Sesso e violenza s'abbandonarono e
si ritrovarono infradiciati quel mattino
glorioso ove tutto cadde a pezzi, e
se saggezza con le sue microscopiche
usanze non ritira truppe dal votarsi
all'angoscia, e se una piccola fierezza
o svista può provocare angosce ritardate
allora cade a pezzi la giornata triste
per la tua feconda grettezza.

Ed è inerme che io battaglio per una
chiarezza che non ha permesso d'esistere
sinché tu giochi con questa providenza
che ci stampò in faccia quell'ansia
di esistere fuori d'un commerciale
attenersi alle più basse voglie; ma
vidi anche nella tua faccia il sigillo
della noncuranza e del vuoto armarsi
alla morte senza pensare alla vita!

the matter: I met you so I'd be obstinately
massacred by you.

And the massacre turns to lust: and
lust in ecstasy contemplated in the
syphilitic corn twisting about
my neck, exhausted by so many abandonments.

Abandoning to empty sex and then seeing
oneself soiled also by the black pitch of
such cramped doings of the poor.

Sex and violence abandoned and found
each other again drenched in that glorious
morning when everything fell to pieces, and
if wisdom with its microscopic customs
doesn't withdraw its troops from turning
to anguish, and if a little pride
or oversight can cause delayed distress
then the sad day falls to pieces
from your fecund stinginess.

And I fight unarmed for a
clarity that isn't permitted to exist
as long as you play with this providence
printing on our face that anxiety
of existing outside of a commercial
sticking to our lowest cravings; but
I also saw in your face the seal
of carelessness and the empty arming
for death without thinking of life!

HANNO TROVATO STRACCI bianchi per terra...

Oh angioli che sommessi e con sommesso ardore
senza vento si coronarono d'amore
ch'io se potessi (e potrò) decantassi
invece di dure realtà a me dure
quello che di gioioso v'è in noi in te
lontana dalla tua selva d'immagini statiche

un nuvolo bianchissimo è più puro amore.

Realtà sempre sfuggì da un'analisi profonda
accorgersi d'essere stato sempre una realtà profonda
i suoi frati requisiti da una coscienza borghese
porta alla conoscenza d'ogni movente
questa realtà che non ha voce in capitolo

le vostre fracassate teste e case.

THEY FOUND WHITE rags on the ground...

Oh angels who subdued and with subdued ardor
windless crowned themselves with amour
that if I could (and would) I'd decant
instead from harsh realities harsh for me
what's joyful in us in you
far from your wood of static images

a very white cloud is purer love.

Reality always escaped from a profound analysis
realizing it had always been a profound reality
its friars requisitioned by a bourgeois conscience
leads to the knowledge of every motive
this reality that has no say in the matter

your smashed heads and houses.

UN MARE BLU blu blu blu blu, anche verde
sottile lampo e il verde s'accende a
volte e v'è giallo il muro di biscotto
e v'è una duna per i tuoi piedi.

Biondo il muro i tuoi occhi
e non v'è
quasi furberia rimasta nel lasciarsi
perdere nel vento acuto che smorza l'incesto
in causa.

E causa è, e causa non è e non v'è terreno
dove non passi l'ottusa mente stancata.

Tua presenza è chiodo infisso e valanghe
di giuramenti non ti tengono a posto:
ruote libere hanno danneggiato il meccanismo
della mia libertà.

A BLUE BLUE blue blue blue sea, even green
thin lightning and the green lights up at
times and there's yellow the cookie wall
and there's a dune for your feet.

Blond the wall your eyes
and there's almost
no mischief left in letting
go in the sharp wind that dampens the incest
in question.

And the question is and isn't and there's no land
where the tired obtuse mind wouldn't go.

Your presence is infixation and floods
of oaths don't make you feel right:
free wheelings have damaged the mechanism
of my freedom.

LIBERTÀ DI PERDERSI nel rotto callo del
piede arrossato dalle libagioni eccelse;
ruota libera ha danneggiato, acceso il
mio annaspare alla libertà.

Libertà d'una serenità che non vuol essere
altro che completa confusione nella
natura ma essa crudele non è fatta per
le nostre scarpate.

E viola e verde e tiranneggiante essa
ancora ordina una muta soggezione a
leggi che hanno per tutto freno la libidine
dei forti e le loro bravate.

FREEDOM TO LOSE oneself in the split callus of
the foot reddened by lofty libations;
free wheeling has damaged, lit my
fumbling for freedom.

Freedom of a serenity that doesn't want to be
other than complete confusion in
nature but cruel it's not made for
our footing.

And purple and green and oppressive it
still orders a silent subjection to
laws that have as sole restraint the lust
of the strong and their feats.

CONTARE I PRIGIONIERI: essi hanno bocche
tutte eguali, larghe falde aperte
tutte eguali! –

E tutte eguali sono le loro bocche che
hanno grappoli invidiosi agli angoli
hanno risa sprovvedute agli orli
dei denti.

Povera miccia: essa ha acceso la polvere
innestata, i suoi doveri
vengono meno all'idea di suicidarsi.

Counting the prisoners: their mouths
are all the same, wide open flaps
all the same!—

And their mouths are all the same
with envious clusters at the corners
with awkward laughter at the edges
of their teeth.

Poor fuse: it has lit the grafted
powder, its duties
give up on the idea of suicide.

TU NON ERI pronta
non essendo pronta riflettevi
non v'era caso più pietoso che il tuo
strillare dal profondo
affranta dal doppio gioco.

Un mercato! ottima mercantessa! diventerò!
padrone di casa che murava gli obblighi
una madre coscienziosa un padre almanacco
sempre lo stesso volto a volteggiare
apparato respiratorio trafugato dall'estero
la fame totale e costante.

È violenza anche carnale: tu corri
disapprodato e io ti rincorro con questo
bel marchio in mano.

You weren't ready
not being ready you considered
there was no case more pitiful than your
screaming from the depths
distraught from the double cross.

A market! great merchant! I'll become!
landlord who walled in the obligations
a conscientious mother an almanac father
always the same face to face
respiratory system smuggled from abroad
total and constant hunger.

It's also carnal violence: you run
unmoored and I chase after you with this
cool brand in hand.

VENTO D'ORIENTE E libeccio di malavita
costipazione d'origine flemmatica; orizzonte
di perle e vita senza forza.

Condividono la mia pena d'essere disarmata
in una strada tutta gas.

Vento d'inverno rabbrividisce d'estate
l'onda della vita ha le sue imprese
venti orrendi tastano la tua fronte
e hai imparato a disamare, finalmente
quando con grandi forbici tastavi un
incontro.

Armata ribelle e voce dall'interno
la libertà soffocata in un sofà
guanti forzati a dimostrarsi maneggevoli
ma avrei voluto prenderlo a pugni
quando lo slacciasti seduto sul sofà
fredda accoglienza a chi ti vuole
verde orario che sempre imbandisce.

WIND EASTERLY AND southwest of the mob
constipation of phlegmatic origin; horizon
of pearls and of drained life.

They share my pain in being disarmed
in a gassed-up street.

Winter wind shudders in summer
the wave of life has its ventures
hideous winds feel your forehead
and you've learned to unlove, finally
when with large cutters you felt an
encounter.

Rebel army and voice from within
freedom suffocated in a sofa
gloves forced to prove handy
but I'd wanted to punch it
when you unlaced it sitting on the sofa
cold welcome to the one who wants you
green timetable forever filling up.

Ho sognato libidini che invece hanno
finte remore pasticciando con il vicino,
la pietà che non ha altro angolo visuale
che quello di ingigantire le promesse,
un avvenire che è uguale a quel passato
spossato.

E te cerco sul binario spossato, e te cerco
nella campagna svuotata.

Dame svuotate... Che pianto!
(fra le tue braccia allargate)
piccola giostra nella spossatezza
che ti riguardava...

Ho nelle braccia formicolanti tutta la forza
di un avvenire coinvolto nel tuo che è assenza
di peso e di noia,
e nell'immenso calderone dei nuvoloni una
peste di canti svogliati.

Essa è deliberatamente impegnata
(nell'immenso sorriso del cielo)
vele rimaneggiate
buona partita di calcio.

Nelle tue braccia abbandonate alla polvere
il torto ch'io subii tastandoti.

I DREAMED OF lust that has instead
feigned qualms meddling with the neighbor,
pity that has no other visual angle
than magnifying promises,
a future that's equal to that spent
past.

And I look for you on the spent track, and I look
for you in the emptied countryside.

Emptied ladies… What a cry!
(in your outstretched arms)
small carousel in the emptiness
that was about you…

In my tingling arms I've all the strength
of a future involved in yours which is absence
of weight and boredom,
and in the immense cauldron of clouds a
plague of listless songs.

She's firmly committed
(in the immense smile of the sky)
reshuffled sails
great soccer game.

In your arms abandoned to dust
the wrong I suffered feeling you.

LA TUA BUIA fronte
fuoco di erbe e di capitali,
danze di bolle di sapone
entrare nella cucina e non vedere più la propria moglie
o invece disertare il corso di guida
coltivare le piante e maledire le stelle
e in una tragedia ritrovarsi, e in
un verso biasimarsi
dedicati purtroppo ad una volontà di
vivere che rasenta il caos
e in un mare di sangue ritrovarsi.

Brusco mutamento di rotta
una causa che ha tutta l'aria di
voler travolgere anche noi
(parola che non smuove altro che aria
infetta).

Accettiamo di noi l'inconscia libertà
scorpacciata
d'infelici nodi nella sua gola arsa
vittoriosa sembra giocare con l'azzardo
che infine si presenta denudato
presentiamoci vittoriosi e denunciatori
di una realtà se è questa quella
per cui non combattiamo
il giorno
che non ci fu dato altro.

Vinse il migliore nei peggiori dei modi
io ero in cantina a lavare i panni
sporchi tuoi.

Your dark forehead
fire of herbs and capitals,
soap bubbles dancing
entering the kitchen and no longer seeing your wife
or instead forsaking the driving school
cultivating plants and cursing stars
and finding yourself in a tragedy, and in
one way blaming yourself
unfortunately dedicated to a will to
live bordering on chaos
and finding yourself in a sea of blood.

Abrupt change of course
a cause that has every intention of
wanting to overwhelm us too
(word that moves nothing but infected
air).

We who accept the unconscious liberty
binging
on unhappy knots in its parched victorious
throat it seems to flirt with gambling
that finally shows itself naked
let's show ourselves victorious and whistleblowers
of a reality if this is the one
we don't fight for
the day
that we were given nothing else.

The best won in the worst ways
I was in the basement airing your
dirty laundry.

IN UN INCONTRO stanco e blu
dovuto all'effusione di giornali
eppure avrei voluto
dipingerle tutte

e io con la forza.

In a tired and blue encounter
due to the effusion of newspapers
I still wanted
to paint them all

and myself by force.

Ho distinto tra la vostra morte e la mia;
la mia non ha spazio: ha divisioni
speciali per chi marca il passo.

Ho varie volte deciso
di non dar ascolto agli indecisi!
dissembrare le mie manie
fare di me stessa un algoritmo, un'alga marina
i miei resti
in un albergo stanziato dai più poveri.

Mai potei perdonare
il suo acume di uomo doloroso
ragionare in un'altra maniera:

avrei voluto disincagliare
dalle nostre paranoiche prestazioni,
le troppo larghe delte della mia infanzia.
Ho assaporato
invece una brutta maniera di vivere,
l'erba dissidente fra i piedi arruffati.
Ho anche promosso a mia scala di valori
infanzia e progenitori.

Come la notte
montagna chiusa nel suo becco duro
non esita a denunciare,
reperire ad uso meno infame
veloce rattristare l'orgoglio
l'ho rimosso dal mio campo d'azione.

Al sorgere di un sole puntiglioso
hai distinto dal tuo distinguere

I DISTINGUISHED BETWEEN your death and mine;
mine has no space: it has special
divisions for marching in place.

Many times I decided
to pay no heed to the undecided!
dissembling my manias
make myself an algorithm, marine algae
my remains
in a hotel allocated to the poorest.

I could never forgive
his acumen of painful man
his reasoning in another way:

I wanted to extricate
from our paranoid performances,
the oversized deltas of my childhood.
I savored
instead an ugly way of life,
the dissident grass under my shaggy feet.
On my scale of values I also promoted
childhood and ancestors.

Much as the night,
a mountain enclosed in its hard beak,
doesn't hesitate to denounce,
to procure for a less shameful use
quick saddening I removed
pride from my field of action.

At the rising of a punctilious sun
you distinguished from your distinguishing

desideri nascosti tra le braccia
una precisa agonia
nell'erba sminuirsi questa agonia
sciupa il nodo della questione.

desires hidden in your arms
a precise agony
demeaning itself in the grass this agony
spoils the crux of the matter.

UNA SOLITUDINE QUADRATA,
considerazioni di fallimento, fallimentare
era l'innocua presenza dell'artista
l'inevitabile programmazione.

E vuole il mondo ch'io difenda
la microscopica vena del tuo ventre
vene misericordiose della
pietà offesa, offensiva –
rullo chiaro nella mia immaginazione
immaginazioni febbrili d'uno
stato devastato, quale libertà impregnata
di odori di stalla.

Vi lanciavamo dalla finestra occlusa
una reale voglia di vendette
scartate a priori
disfarsi anche della vendetta
e poi hanno disdetto
l'ultimo appuntamento.

Quale voce cauta mi prese, quale
ombra triste, non
l'ombra del pane ai denti
ma la sua propria essenza!

E forte volle anche la sua essenza
si liberava del profitto per ricadere
nell'essenza: rispondere a domande
mentre rastrellavano i maiali
se nell'edificio crollava la vena ironica
i suoi pensieri (povera roba sfruttata)
un gran raggiro di mele.

A SQUARED SOLITUDE,
considerations of failure, failed
was the artist's innocuous presence
the inevitable programming.

And the world wants me to defend
the microscopic vein of your womb
merciful veins of the
offended, offensive piety—
clear scroll in my imagination
feverish imaginings of a devastated
state, like liberty impregnated
with the smell of the stable.

We threw you from the occluded window
a real desire for revenge
discarded a priori
getting rid of revenge too
and then they reneged on
their last appointment.

Which cautious voice took me, which
sad shadow, not
the shadow you sank your teeth into
but its own essence!

And strong she wanted her essence too
she got rid of the profit to fall back
into the essence: answering questions
while they raked the pigs
if the ironic vein collapsed in the building
her thoughts (poor exploited stuff)
a great scam of apples.

RIMAI, VERSO UNA proda
e mi ritiravo sull'orlo
invece tutto si faceva passato lugubre
una impreparata decisione
di afferrare con ambo le mani la decisione
nelle mie mani sanguinose
per le pratiche quotidiane.

Un rosso ardore
svuotata ogni forma dal suo perfetto
senso,
e sui velodromi correvano le piste
per il futuro furto di anime umane.

Riparare
più vicino al mare
placida esistenza non riparata
dalle bombe a mano,
placido shock che risorge
dalla sua abituale placidità
veneree discussioni di principio
i contendenti una rivolta che partecipa
a tutta la tragicità della comicità
tra gli alberi del mare.

Quale vuoto
hai voluto portare in questo vuoto
con desiderio di fuga e di vuoto
a capire il perché del furto.

I RHYMED, TOWARD a bank
and I retreated to the brink
instead all became mournful past
an unprepared decision
to grasp the decision with both hands
in my bloody hands
for my daily practices.

A red ardor
emptied every form from its perfect
sense,
and the tracks ran around the velodromes
for the future theft of human souls.

Sheltering
closer to the sea
placid existence unsheltered
from hand grenades,
placid shock arising
from its usual placidity
venereal discussions of principle
the contenders a revolt participating
in the whole tragedy of comedy
among the arbors of the sea.

Which void
did you want to carry into this void
with a desire for escape and void
to understand the reason for the theft.

FIANCHEGGIANDO IL VUOTO albero le tende
delle formiche parevano ricordare quale
follia fosse esistere. Aveano ricche
colonne di sostituti scaraventatisi
nella prurigine della scorza virulenta
come un divino dio.

Ho visto fuori marcarsi di saliva ogni
mio sforzo al gioco che mal tornava
in ondulazioni verdi.

Quale foresta di ignari abeti ristorava
le mie perdute forze?

E in cima agli alberi muoiono a volte
gli scoiattoli arcigni nel calibro di
una lunga coda; il folto stringere di
proliferi archi e spine non ha necessariamente
alcun significato. Ma ho visto anche
tornar comodo il sacrificarsi di animali
e non è sempre un beneficio fare da
maremma agli umiliati cervi vinti dal
freddo.

Questionando la natura vidi solo un
passo falso: quello dell'uomo invidioso
della materna natura che castrandosi
obbedì ai primordiali istinti. Hanno
abbattuto ogni sorta di placida occasione
al vivificarsi mite della vita che coronandosi
di successi non poté oltre sopportare
la squallida vicenda degli esiliati.
Ed hanno aperto maschere a così involontario

FLANKING THE EMPTY tree the ants'
tents seemed to remember what
madness it was to exist. They had rich
columns of substitutes flung out
in the itch of the virulent rind
like a godly god.

Outside I saw my every effort marking
itself with saliva at the game going badly
in green undulations.

Which forest of unsuspecting firs restored
my lost strength?

And sometimes they die on the treetops
the grim squirrels within the caliber of
a long tail; the thick grip of
proliferous arches and thorns hasn't necessarily
any meaning. But I've also seen
the sacrifice of animals come in handy
and it's not always beneficial to provide a
maremma for the humiliated deer defeated by the
cold.

Questioning nature I saw only one
false step: that of the envious man
of maternal nature who castrating himself
obeyed primordial instincts. They
destroyed all sorts of placid occasions
at the meek vivification of life that crowning itself
with successes could no longer bear
the squalid vicissitudes of the exiled.
And they opened masks to such an involuntary

volere la pace in terra. Quale mai fu
l'ingegno arido che tanti ostacoli pose

ad un più ricco salvaguardarsi? È forse
vinta la vita e non ha specie risoltesi
a combattere il male.

wish for peace on earth. What could it have been
this arid genius that put so many obstacles

in the way of a richer safeguard? Maybe
life is defeated and has no species resolved
to fight evil.

E HO VISTO che sollevandomi di peso
le sillabe non mostrano altro che una
passata confermazione ad un ordine
prestabilito (tutte le mie vanità al
punto tale da non trarre in inganno).
Ho inteso infatti il verde come un
mangiacolori e ho verificato il volo
delle cicogne, abbassando le ali durante
il volo e tralasciando di prendere in
considerazione anche la tua lealtà.
Ho voluto scappare con le bagatelle
e ho scambiato un mostro con una tarantella
confinata nei miei approcci letterari
ad una turbe immensa e ordinaria. Ho
visto io con i miei occhi il mio linguaggio
farsi rasoterra e decifrabile: ma non
è così sovente che si sposta, la terra
dalle sue ruote indenni.

E ho iscritto nella mia bilancia fragile
una frase che mi fa di tua appartenenza
mentre con facili virtù disgiungevi
ogni tua reale appartenenza al fiore
della montagna infreddolita che si stende
ai piedi del primo che si possa dire
vinto.

AND I'VE SEEN syllables lifting me up
that show nothing but one
past confirmation of a predetermined
order (all my vanities to the
point of not being misleading).
I meant of course green as a
color-eater and I verified the flight
of storks, lowering my wings during
the flight and refusing to take into
consideration your loyalty too.
I wanted to run away with a bagatelle
and I mistook a monster for a tarantella
confined in my literary approaches
to an immense and ordinary throng. I've
seen with my own eyes my language
become low-level and intelligible: but it's
not often that the earth moves
from its unscathed wheels.

And I inscribed in my fragile scale
a phrase that makes me belong to you
while with easy virtue you disjoined
your every real belonging to the cold
mountain flower stretching out
at the feet of the first who lays claim to
defeat.

DELIRAI, IMPERFETTA, SU scale
di bastoni
cose di cucina, casa e
impellenti misure che
ti riconoscono l'abilità alle manovre.

L'erborista
mal si conteneva
cannibali si distinsero
per una sorta di selvaggia trasparenza
ma i tuoi grandi occhi
non versano in mal celato affetto altro
che stridenti colorazioni,
semplici abbandoni nel parcheggio affondato.

Trent'anni sono un lasso di tempo conveniente
per ritirare la mano dal fuoco umido
e stringere a sé i bambini che adoro
mentre fuori puzzavano vini inaciditi
un'unità
di cui disconosci le proprietà.

Trovai una pietra bagnata di lacrime
il suo soave splendore un
poco rovinato dalle palestre,
giuro di amare il catasto
nel suo gingillare per il perdono
nel pedigree delle destinazioni.

Se esco e faccio la spesa
orrore si fracassa appena
belle cicogne snelle
m'assembrano le membra.

I RAVED, IMPERFECT, on a ladder
of clubs
kitchen implements, home and
compelling measures that
acknowledge your ability to maneuver.

The herbalist
barely restrained himself
cannibals stood out
for a sort of savage transparency
but your big eyes
spill nothing with ill-concealed affection
but strident colorations,
simple abandon in the sunken parking lot.

Thirty years is sufficient time
to withdraw my hand from the moist fire
and hold the children I adore
while outside turned wine stank
a unity
whose properties you deny.

I found a stone wet with tears
its gentle splendor a
bit roughed up by the gyms,
I swear to love the land registry
in its trifling with forgiveness
in the pedigree of destinations.

If I go to the store
horror barely shatters
beautiful slender storks
assemble my limbs.

NOTTE, LABIRINTO SORTEGGIATO
chilometri a volte ti dividono
dal rotondo occhio del vicino
fiori fiacchi nella mia mente
la distanza che separa
il vuoto coronarsi di successi
gli oliveti.

Con quel suo bel colore arancione
indeciso era tra tentazioni
è meglio farla finita con la fame,
bastonando i poveri cani
gatti impregnati di un sottile odore
che era la tua figura satanica o saggia.
Ha verde seme il bilancio della stagione
e io ho verde rimpianto
Cristo con le sue lumache
ha disperazione a tinte rosa
e blu profondo
«Inno alla vita sul punto di morte»
la sezione è un bidone.

Coronata di successo la mia
opera si fece; per anni in camerini
lo studioso grezzo impazziva
di malinconia.

NIGHT, DRAWN LABYRINTH
kilometers sometimes divide you
from the round eye of your neighbor
floppy flowers in my mind
the distance that separates
the empty crowning of achievements
the olive groves.

With that beautiful orange color
torn between temptations
it's better to do away with hunger,
clubbing the poor dogs
cats impregnated with a subtle smell
that was your figure satanic or wise.
The season's outcome has green seed
and I have green regret
Christ with his snails
has despair in shades of pink
and deep blue
"Hymn to life on the verge of death"
the section is a deception.

My work was crowned
with success; for years in dressing rooms
the rustic scholar went mad
from melancholy.

PINI HANNO MARE accanto e calda sabbia
hanno rospi i rivoli e hanno ombra gelida
alla mia accaldata coscienza: ma malinconia
sembra smuovere ben poco di quel che
tanto s'arrischia a sembrar morte.

Hanno fuoco i pini e disastrose conseguenze
hanno le alte mani alzate a benedire
un così tacito cielo spalmato con ingegno
e disperazione. Quale disperazione può
mai pensare di trovare l'onnipossente

in quella manciata di erbe alte?

Hanno vissuto ore migliori gli scavi
che abbronzando il paesaggio sembrano
dirti sempre addio a miglior vita! E

voglia e noia sembrano costantemente
prenderti per la manica nella gelatina
delle ore serali.

Non ho accesso io a tanto paradiso e
non possono commuovermi i piani tenuti
per tanto tempo segreti da neri comandanti
che sorreggevano la sorte del mondo!

Vuol comandare il mondo la sua stanca
motocicletta e digrigna i denti tesi
nel supremo sforzo.

PINES HAVE SEA nearby and warm sand
rivulets have toads and cast an icy shadow
on my hot conscience: but melancholy
seems to stir very little of what
dares so much it seems like death.

Pines have fire and disastrous consequences
their hands raised high to bless
such a silent sky spread with genius
and despair. What despair can
ever think of finding the almighty

in that handful of tall grasses?

They've seen better hours the excavations
that tanning the landscape always seem
to bid you farewell to a better life! And

desire and boredom as if constantly
tugging you by the sleeve in the gelatin
of the evening hours.

I have no access to so much heaven and
can't be moved by plans kept secret
for so long by black commanders
who weighed the fate of the world!

Her tired motorbike wants to rule
the world grinding its teeth tensed
in supreme effort.

AH COME I merli tacciono! Hanno confuso
la tua idea della tristezza con una confusa
sordità ai bisogni degli altri, con
una totale guerra agli impulsi più benigni
confondendo la tua bontà con tristi
pini benigni.

Vuole quel muro così disastroso, perenne
nella sua stolida camerateria, che tu
non trova altra benigna pietà fuori
delle tue terre astruse.

E nell'alcova covano rospi un loro tragico
destino d'essere ingannati dai topi
che stolidamente marciando per vie traverse
hanno marcato la tua vita di ruggine.

Ruggine avversa, e fiocchi di neve nei
nuvoli che mai dorati languono su rive
ventilate in un cielo pronto a redimersi
per una qualsiasi questione appariscente
mentre con le mani affusolate rischi
d'imbellettare troie mancate. Un matrimonio
di audaci piani, una riviera silenziosa
di morte: un tuono nel cielo che prepara
ogni tua infanzia.

Ha il cielo una moltitudine di ombre
ha il cielo una mano agghiacciata, e
novo ordine mai sparse vita con tanto
ardore.

AH HOW QUIET are the blackbirds! They confused
your notion of sadness with a confused
deafness to the needs of others, with
an all-out war on the most benign impulses
confusing your good will with the sad
benign pines.

That disastrous wall, perennial
in its stolid camaraderie, wishes that you
find no other benign piety beyond
your abstruse lands.

And in the alcove toads hatch their tragic
destiny to be deceived by mice
that marching stolidly along side streets
marked your life with rust.

Adverse rust, and snowflakes in the
never gilded clouds languish on ventilated
banks in a sky ready to redeem itself
for just about any conspicuous issue
while with tapering hands you risk
embellishing would-be whores. A marriage
of audacious plans, a quiet river
of death: a thunderbolt in the sky preparing
your every childhood.

The sky has a multitude of shadows
the sky has a frozen hand, and
a new order never strewed life with so much
ardor.

VENTO CHE HA viscide tracce in un deserto
pieno di ruvide scene: piccole ondulazioni
nella sabbia scrostata e nelle finte
scene folleggia la parte che io ho di
me, nell'ottobre autunnale o notturno.

Ed ha rima incerta il coltivare segrete
speranze e dimore!

Ma smuove a vita un inorgoglito strano
odiarsi e opporsi a quello che di calmo
vi è in loro, i nostri fanciulli desolati
e consci della loro forza.

Ha verde maligna forza quel corpo d'ombre
dentro la sottile preghiera: e semplice
assembraggio di resti è semplice disfatta
ai loro occhi tumefatti. Come facilitare
al fuoco la grandine? Violentemente
scardina la porta, al mio cuore consolatorio.

WIND WITH SLIMY traces in a desert
full of rough scenes: small undulations
in the stripped sand and in the fake
scenes the part I have of myself revels,
in this autumnal or nocturnal October.

And my secret hopes and dwellings
have uncertain rhyme!

But this stirs to life a proud strange
hating of one another and opposing whatever
calmness is in them, our desolate youngsters
conscious of their strength.

It exudes evil green strength that body of shadows
inside the subtle prayer: and simple
assembling of remains is simple defeat
in their bitten eyes. How to help
the hail to the fire? Violently
it unhinges the door, to my consoling heart.

TENDE RIVOLUZIONARIE NEL mio cuore
coltivando in segreto piccole manie,
conveniente ci sembrò l'alba misteriosa
in atti particolari osceni nel giardino
pubblico.

Vola nel vuoto questo mio oblioso cuore
avrà gèmito il mio squilibrato ardore
un vento scamiciato nella sua angolosità
da debutto.

Fratello che non ha curva interiore
hanno verdi tende le sequele di nastri
tagliàti col forbice d'una vena artistica
e salienti i tuoi tratti imprimono
sul colle dignitoso mani, tuo trono
comincia con lo spolverare mani asciutte
o bianche.

E in amare mani sproloquiare in felici
visioni d'una tranquilla morte spronare
le vesti silenziose del tuo passato
hanno visto muoversi in un'ombra dolce
e cara la tetra salma di venti vite
spese in vano.

Revolutionary tents in my heart
secretly nurturing small manias,
it seemed convenient to us the mysterious dawn
in particular obscene acts in the public
garden.

My oblivious heart flies into the void
my deranged ardor will moan
a sleeveless wind in its debut
angularity.

Brother lacking an inner curve
the sequences of ribbons feature green tents
cut with scissors of an artistic vein
and your salient features impress
hands on the dignified hill, your throne
starts with dusting dry or white
hands.

And in bitter hands raving in happy
visions of a quiet death spurring
the silent garments of your past
they saw moving in a sweet and dear
shadow the dismal remains of twenty lives
spent in vain.

FIORI DENUDATI E stonati nell'umile
facilità al pianto che hanno questi
ingarbugliati versi o fiori: portami
la tua sequenza di immaginazioni, ho
sorriso e lamentato anche disastrose
conseguenze alla mia sensibilità di
Venere stordita dalle campagne pubblicitarie.

Ne parve cambiata così come un ippodromo
curva ad ogni speranza.

Furia nello sguardo e consistente arrivismo
grande abbaglio, di vini a poco prezzo
così come la tua veste.

FLOWERS STRIPPED AND tuneless in the humble
talent for crying of these tangled
lines or flowers: bring me
your sequence of imaginations, I
smiled and also complained of disastrous
consequences to my sensitivity of a
Venus stunned by advertising campaigns.

She seemed to have changed much as a racetrack
turns at every hope.

Fury in the eye and stable careerism
big blunder, of cheap wines
along with your garments.

CAVALLI CONSISTENTI SORVEGLIATI da
un agente hanno lanciato bombe a gas
continuamente in movimento.

Hanno volontari che assembrano i resti
e poi li montano su un camioncino così
come tutte le nostre prove d'amore
falliscono.

Con successi profondamente negati alla
più parte della gente s'accorse d'essere
dalla parte giusta.

E nelle mani contenere a pugno chiuso
una quantità di biglietti da mille
che vergognandosi risposero al silenzio
con immagazzinate qualità. Vero è il
fumo, offre con la sua consolazione
l'elettrico ballo di San Vito.

Perché hanno questi fiori e questi
nomi tanto tempo a disposizione urtandosi
contro le pareti della stanza?

Volitiva si spiegazzò indenne nell'interno
dell'appartamento rosa.

Stable horses guarded by
an officer hurled gas bombs
in continuous motion.

They've volunteers assembling the remains
and then mounting them up on a pickup
the way all our proofs of love
fail.

With successes profoundly denied to
most she realized she was
on the right side.

And holding in her hands
with clenched fist a stack of bills
that feeling ashamed answered the silence
with well-stocked qualities. True is the
smoke, it offers with its consolation
an electric Saint Vitus' dance.

Why do these flowers and
names spend so much time bumping
into each other and against the walls?

Strong willed she wrinkled unscathed inside
the pink apartment.

ED HANNO SOFFICI manti quei ragazzi
imprigionati nelle loro sostanze: verniciate
folte chiome. Versano acqua nell'emporio
buono a tutto: la libidine. Essa ha
cangianti colori foschi e gialli convenientemente
ridotti ad un livello immaginario a
sua soddisfazione privata.

Hanno sondato tutte le possibili sonde
e hanno forti del loro avere scelto
odori minaccianti colorati di dispetti
e anche spesso di valutazioni errate.

Nella Pearl Harbor che sono io esprimersi
mai ebbe a miglior sorte altro che
vanagloriosa espulsione dei resti, il
lavoratore non per questo distratto
dalla sua missione: che era oligarchica,
e sentenziosa, mentre dietro alle finestre
stringeva il mazzo di rose. Oltraggiò
pubblicamente la bestia, promosse una
crocifissione di così minor conto da
drasticamente contaminarne l'ambiente.

Mossa dal vento in piccoli grappoli
redivivi dalla parte sbagliata sopperire
ma con placide finestrelle tu hai invece
decolorato il cielo, stesso e steso
nella lavanderia delle nostre buon anime.

Chiusi in un sacco gli impiegati cominciarono
a rendere ragione delle loro azioni
e non erano poche quelle che turbavano.

And those kids have soft coats
imprisoned in their substances: painted
thick mane. They pour water into the emporium
good-for-everything: pure lust. It's got
pied bleak and yellow colors conveniently
reduced to an imaginary level for
its private satisfaction.

They probed all possible probes
and thanks to their choice they have
colorful threatening odors of teasing
and also often faulty estimates.

In the Pearl Harbor that I am expression
never met a better fate than that
vainglorious expulsion of the remains, the
worker undistracted by this
from his mission—oligarchic
and sententious—while behind the windows
he clasped the bouquet of roses. He publicly
insulted the beast, he promoted a
crucifixion so minor as to
drastically contaminate the environment.

Moved by the wind in small bunches
revived the wrong way compensating
but with tiny placid windows you've bleached
the sky instead, alike and aloft
in the laundry of our good souls.

Locked in a bag the employees started
to account for their actions
and the troublesome were far from few.

CONDURRE CON SÉ gli impiegati
fronteggiare l'impreveduto
impossibili attitudini
scoperte di avanguardie scoperte
confinate nella notte d'una vecchia
conoscenza; nell'alberazione
d'una quotidiana coscienza.

Quale fracasso assembri
nelle montagne vivaci
pur tacendo. Hai manomesso frontiere

mai ebbi da voi altro che prigioni.

TAKING THE EMPLOYEES with you
facing the unforeseen
impossible attitudes
discoveries of discovered avant-gardes
confined in the night of an old
acquaintance; in the arboring
of a daily conscience.

What hubbub you assemble
in the lively mountains
while keeping mum. You tampered with borders

I had nothing but prisons from you.

L'INACCETTABILE REALTÀ
manipola così bene la realtà
ogni
cosa attorno o dentro mentre con cose

terra che fra le tue
ginocchia non poteva crescere nello
spazio

un fine gioco che è d'un altro giro
compatrioti
stanchi, la pallida
èra dei nostri trasporti
visibile a vista un continuo getto di
grattacieli

UNACCEPTABLE REALITY
manipulates reality so well
every
thing around or within while with things

earth that between your
knees couldn't grow into
space

an endgame from another round
tired
compatriots, the pale
age of our transportations
visible in view a continuous stream of
skyscrapers

Hanno fuso l'ordigno di guerra con le
mie dita troppo occupate a servirsi
di cibi cannibaleschi e tutto il mondo
è corso a vedere.

Pene infranto e rotta condotta sono
lì a farvi da guida: l'esperienza è
maestra degli svogliati, i poveri d'immaginazione
che rotolandosi nell'aldilà hanno voluto

imprigionarvi. Voglia di fare temprata
da consuetudini che hanno invece tremebonde
pratiche: quelle di non sapere dove
le hanno lasciate.

Ed è il dovere a farti strada come fosse
una sbiadita lanterna e spaccata che
nulla illumina salvo che il tuo piede
che sbaglia.

Gli aeroplani hanno cominciato a sparare
sulla folla poi hanno tradito così come
è normale nella pioggia di ogni giorno
e anche la sera.

Ogni giorno tentano un tranello e ogni
giorno torna la purezza e ogni notte
mettono in dubbio quello che hanno fatto
di giorno.

Di giorno sognano; di notte vegliano;
il pomeriggio dormono; la mattina pregano.

THEY MELTED THE war device with my
fingers too busy to have
cannibalistic foods and the whole world
ran to see.

Shattered penis and broken conduct are
there to guide you: experience is
the master of the listless, the poor in imagination
that rolling in the afterlife wanted

to imprison you. Desire to act tempered
by habits that instead have trembling
practices: of not knowing where
they left them.

And it's duty leading you as if it were
a cracked and faded lantern that
illuminates nothing except your foot's
missteps.

Airplanes had started shooting
at a crowd then betrayal as
is normal in everyday rain
and even in the evening.

Every day they try a trap and every
day purity returns and every night
they question what they did
by day.

They dream by day; keep watch by night;
in the afternoon they sleep; in the morning pray.

Pregano che non se n'andrà così presto
la vita che ha nascosto la morte per
tanto tempo finché un giorno ritrovarono
la notte stesa come un morto.

They pray that it won't leave so soon
the life that for so long
hid death until one day they found
the night laid out like one dead.

VIENE
soffiata giù per le scale,
similitudine ch'io faccio di ogni cosa
che passa per la mente
come se fosse sempre pronto lì il perdono.

Barattare le sigarette altrui
per una mansarda piena di buoni libri...

Ho visto nella curia e nelle percentuali
stendersi il processo tra le righe
e io ho assolto il comandante
perché tu eri il solito massacratore

di donne nel labirinto
spaventate dal grido
tra montagne di roccia
nell'orrore di una bomba
non scoppiata

come tutte le nostre cose migliori:
politica nella sua dozzinale vendita
largisci i tuoi poteri assembrati
tra gli analfabeti del quartiere

e tra la polvere che tu portavi intatta
nel grigio bagaglio.

It's
blown down the stairs,
the likeness that I find in all things
that comes to mind
as if forgiveness were always right there.

Trading others' cigarettes
for a loft stuffed with good books...

I've seen in the curia and in the percentages
the trial laid out between the lines
and I've acquitted the commander
because you were the usual slaughterer

of women in the maze
frightened by the scream
between rocky mountains
in the horror of an undetonated
bomb

like all our best things:
politics with its cheap pitches
you extend your assembled powers
among the neighborhood illiterate

and in the dust that you carried intact
in your gray baggage.

UNA TUA FACCIA ha sì contorni umani
un tuo gesto è davvero primaverile e
un tuo guardarmi è la prima delle cose

a cui penso quando – nel vivido primeggiare
dei nuvoli pomeridiani – io con molta
lentezza cerco te.

E se il morire è cosa di ogni giorno
anche il tuo sguardo ha luci maligne
e un tuo cenno di timidezza o d'amore

non fa altro che ritardare l'orrore
di un giorno.

ONE FACE OF yours has such human contours
one gesture from you is truly like spring and
your looking at me is the first thing

I think of when—in the vivid springing forth
of the afternoon clouds—most
slowly I seek you.

And if dying is daily fare
even your eyes have evil lights
and one hint of shyness or love from you

does nothing but delay the horror
of a day.

QUESTO È IL mare oggi
in ondate più serene che squarciano
quel tuo grido e quel tuo affanno deliberatamente

fondendosi la
visione di uno strazio con uno strazio
tutto si rifà,

e da capo e di nuovo

THIS IS THE sea today
with calmer waves ripping
your cry and your anxiety deliberately

merging the
vision of a torment with a torment
everything is redone,

afresh and anew

ANCHE LUI HA impiccato la rivoluzione
vorresti farla finita con le grandezze
un bene ne chiama un altro e con semplicità
(revisionata all'una di notte e con

insonnia) distruggi un bricciolo
di quel che vorresti distruggere.

Il fondo della giornata è quella
hanno voluto celebrare il
quinto anniversario della vittoria
hanno convinto perfino te che tu sei andata
ad annegare, tutti
attorno non vincevano, ma perivano.

Sono periti a dozzine
tu perirai l'indomani

se tu voli,
e ti battezzo nemico del popolo.

Frase non semplice
tocca a te farne a meno
e così disfare
quella lezione che mi hai dato di praticità
e in orario mostrarti che anche io ho
fede nella ragione.

Esistevano vuoti e vani nella mia mente
versi fatti con furore di distrazione
mostrano che per ultimo v'era questo
pezzo di carta.

HE TOO HANGED the revolution
you'd like to be done with greatness
one good turn deserves another and with simplicity
(revised at one in the morning and with

insomnia) you destroy a shred
of what you'd like to destroy.

The bottom of the day is that one
they wanted to celebrate the
fifth anniversary of the victory
they convinced even you that you'd gone
to drown, no one
nearby won, but perished.

Dozens perished
you'll perish the next day

if you fly,
and I baptize you the enemy of the people.

Not a simple sentence
it's up to you to do without it
and thus undoing
that lesson in practicality you gave me
and showing you punctually that I too have
faith in reason.

Verses made in a furor of distraction
existed empty and vain in my mind
they show that in the end there was this
piece of paper.

Ho venti giorni
per fare una rivoluzione: ho
altri venti giorni dopo la rivoluzione
per conoscermi
mio piccolo diario sentenzioso.

Tana per
le fresche menti
le parole,
un pugno
chiuso che le garantisce
la mia più imbattibile ragione d'essere.

Il nemico le strappa le vesti
la felicità è un micro-organismo nell'interno
dell'infelicità

nel cimitero
non sa smettere di essere felice.

I'VE TWENTY DAYS
to start a revolution: I've
another twenty days after the revolution
to get to know myself
my sententious little diary.

Den of
fresh minds
words,
a clenched
fist that ensures
my most compelling reason for being.

The enemy tears off her clothes
happiness is a micro-organism within
unhappiness

in the cemetery
she can't help feeling happy.

QUELLO SCORRERE PRIMARIO distrutto
i suoi petali che camminano a ritroso
e la rabbia di morire
nella vita non ha limite.

Il mio tirassegno di piccole perle bendate
(viene un vuoto a pensarci)
sono io a dissolverlo
era fatto di tempo prezioso.

Nell'occhio lamentevole fingere
quel dozzinale amarsi:
pudore della banalità
collasso tutto ad un tratto:

il rosso accendisigaro,
questa è una visione interiore
povera di intendimento
ma salvata da questi colori.

THAT PRIMARY DESTROYED flow
its petals walking backwards
and the anger of dying
in life has no limit.

My dartboard of small bandaged pearls
(a blank to think about it)
I'm the one who dissolves it
it was made of precious time.

In the mournful eye pretending
that dime-a-dozen love:
modesty of banality
all of a sudden collapsing:

the red cigarette lighter,
this is an inner vision
lacking in understanding
but saved by these colors.

IL FUOCO S'ARRAMPICA per insoliti rami
e nel verde si nascondono anche piccole
bestie, esse sono le rarità del nostro
pianeta mentre tutte le varianti di
una età di pietra mostrano violenti
scontri e proliferazioni sagaci. Ma
io non ho nella mia mano alcuna erba
medicamentosa, non ho alcuna speranza
di potere un giorno cangiarti a vista
mentre sperimentando con il mio corpo
tu ti accingi a visitarmi, insapiente
mentre neghi ogni altra ricetta alla
tua vanagloria di saperne di più degli
alberi, e più dei fiumi che scorrono
borbottando tra le vigne.

La mia unica erba è questo fumo per
i palazzi separati dai vetri delle alte
finestre ed è fumando che io vedo meglio
di quale stoffa era fatta la nostra credenza
di uno e dell'altro. L'altro con alte
penne ha rigettato l'affetto, l'effetto
di una rosea nube che costringeva a
reperire nell'altro ogni speranza di
gioia.

FIRE SCALES UNCOMMON branches
and in the greenery they hide small
beasts too, they're the rarities of our
planet while all the variants of
a stone age stage violent
clashes and sagacious proliferations. But
I've no medicinal grass
in my hand, I've no hope
of changing you in plain sight one day
while experimenting with my body
you get ready to examine me, unwise
while you deny any other prescription to
your vainglory to know more than
the trees, and more than the rivers that flow
burbling through the vineyards.

My only herb is this smoke along
the buildings divided by tall window
panes and while smoking I better see
of what stuff our credence was made
of one and the other. The other with tall
wings rejected affection, the effect
of a rosy cloud that forced
finding in the other any hope of
joy.

IL FREDDO FA paura e il sangue anche
il mare ha fonti imbalsamate nell'arcano
splendore del suo fallimento: il freddo
ha freddo e il caldo non appare a tradire
i suoi compagni.

Scompagnato il freddo adora la calda
estate ma severamente è proibito staccarsi
dalle cose basse e perciò illuminante
si fa la risorsa del povero: setacciare
l'universo in vista d'un pasto.

Ho freddo oggi e non so perché nel
cuore si setaccia una nuova attitudine:
quella di infischiarsi del domani: ma
non è vero che il domani sia sicuro
e non è vero che l'oggi è calmo.

COLD IS SCARY and blood too
the sea has embalmed springs in the arcane
splendor of its failure: cold
is cold and heat doesn't show up to betray
its mates.

Unmated cold worships the warm
summer but breaking away from base things
is strictly forbidden and thus the resources
of the poor become enlightened: sifting
the universe in view of a meal.

I'm cold today and I don't know why a new
attitude sifts through my heart:
writing off tomorrow: but
it's not true that tomorrow is certain
and it's not true that today is calm.

VERDE RAMO INFUSO nell'accordarsi d'un
ciambellano: una ciambella, un ramo
un cianciare; e non trovo la parola
che elegante non vuol parlare...

Fiori eleganti e il ramo si piega a
destra come fosse fiorito e lordo di
promettenti parole che non escono dall'immagine
che tu ti sei fatta di loro.

Buono l'abete, ancor più buono il ramo
pendente: chili di frutta o fiore lo
appesantiscono: e ancora non ricordi
quell'altro suo nome!

Verdigris-infused branch in accord with a
chamberlain: a chamber, a branch
a chattering; and I can't find a word
so elegant that it doesn't want to talk…

Elegant flowers and the branch bends to
the right as if it were flowery and heavy with
promising words that agree with the picture
you got from them.

The fir is good, the pending branch
even better: piles of fruit or flower
weigh it down: and still you can't remember
its other name!

NON DEVE CADERE in frantumi
è peccato di paura
osservi galleggiare la brace
nella cristallina indecenza del vero
pattuita col diavolo
raro servizio reso al caso
tendersi tra due anime disertate

IT MUSTN'T FALL and shatter
it's the sin of fear
you observe embers floating
in the crystalline indecency of truth
a pact with the devil
rare service offered to the case
extending between two deserted souls

Neve

Sembrano minuscoli insetti festeggianti
uno sciame di motori squillanti, una
pena discissa in faticose attenzioni
e una radunata di bravate.

Nevica fuori; e tutto questo rassomiglia
ad una crisi giovanile di pianto se
non fosse che ora le lacrime sono asciutte
come la neve.

Un esperto di questioni meteorologiche
direbbe che si tratta di un innamoramento
ma io che sono un esperto in queste
cose direi forse che si tratta di una

imboscata!

Snow

They look like tiny celebrant insects
a swarm of shrill engines, a
pain discrete in distracted attentions
and a gathering of stunts.

It's snowing outside; and all of this resembles
a youthful weepiness except
that now tears are dry
as snow.

An expert on meteorological matters
would say that this is a case of falling in love
but being an expert in these
things I'd say maybe it's an

ambush!

MILLE, PICCOLI OGGETTI delicati, la
falce e il martello sono divenuti punti
interrogativi.

La mia vita privata è un best-seller
e i miei romanzi d'amore sono luride facilitazioni
e io ne riconosco l'errore.

La neve scende piana svolazzando contenta
il mio cuore si rabbuia attentamente
si contrae e si perdona con uno schiaffo

fatto su misura. Oh il vento è leggero!
e non vuol disturbare l'ordine della

pace in terra.

A THOUSAND SMALL, delicate objects, the
hammer and sickle have become question
marks.

My private life is a best seller
and my love stories are lurid simplifications
and I acknowledge my error.

The snow falls flatly happily fluttering
my heart darkens carefully
contracting and forgiving itself with a custom-made

slap. Oh the wind is light!
and doesn't want to disturb the order of

peace on earth.

Collasso

Sono i fiocchi di neve decaduti a fare
da augurio ad una vita senza luce e
il loro danzare è tutta una farsa, perché
noi non abbiamo accese le luci.

Sotto le fontane massacranti il male
dilaga, forte di una sua forte ambizione
spinge come il vento i bocconi di neve.

La saggezza è una bara... barare al
gioco ha più scampo che non questo burrascoso
perdersi e ritrovarsi per le vie della
ragione...

Il cielo nevoso è immobile come se avvertisse
di una grandiosa immobile servitù. La
neve ha quasi finito di sperare.

Collapse

It's the fallen snowflakes that serve
as an omen for a life without light and
their dancing is just a farce, because
we haven't turned on the lights.

Under the pummeling fountains evil
spreads, strong in its strong ambition
it pushes like the wind the snow bites.

Wisdom is a casket… cheating at
the game stands more of a chance than this stormy
losing and finding yourself in the ways of
reason…

The snowy sky is still as if it were warning
of a grand still servitude. The
snow has almost given up hope.

MI IMMISCHIAI DI nuovo
la fame ci tenne stretti
essere (pur obbedendo alla natura)
una selvatica accondiscendenza:
misi briglie al collo a quel cavallo:
come se fosse morto.

A tutto spiano verso ignote terre
io non potetti riparare
il guasto fornitomi dal mio cervello
stasi permanente come la neve
divinatoria nel giorno della pioggia.

Felice la mia memoria disegna
sue potenzialità aperte;
inalberata più lontano di
quel mio vaneggiare.

Sismiche scosse ribollono
di ingiustizie
mattiniero invece
il principio della giustizia.

Once more I meddled
hunger held us tight
being (while obeying nature)
a wild condescension:
I bridled that horse's neck:
as if it were dead.

Nonstop toward unknown lands
I couldn't repair
the failure provided by my brain
permanent stasis like divinatory
snow on that day of rain.

Happily my memory designs
its open potential;
hoisted up beyond
my raving.

Seismic shocks boil
with injustices
early riser instead
the principle of justice.

CREDETE DI POTER amarmi? Avete visto in me
dei difetti? Me li toglierei volentieri, in
vostro onore...

Ma non ho visto invece querelarsi invano le
beghe d'ufficio, i sismotici arrivisti, la
nostra giornata grigia e agitata.

Perché hanno steso questi fogli? Perché hanno
fatto mistero delle vendite? Perché questo
mio affanno impreparato?

Ho ordito contro le folle una stampa libera
delle sue proprie azioni e mi travolge un
inconscio bisogno di gloria.

Eppure fu la bellezza a prima ispirare i raggi
di sole improvvisamente spenti dalla tenda
tirata!

You thought you could love me? You saw in me
which defects? I'd gladly get rid of them, in
your honor...

But haven't I seen though the office quarrels
suing themselves in vain, the seismic
careerists, our gray and agitated day.

Why did they draft these sheets? Why did
they make the sales a secret? Why this
unprepared anxiety of mine?

I plotted against the crowds a press free
of its own actions and an unconscious
need for glory overcame me.

Yet it was beauty that first inspired the rays
of the sun suddenly extinguished by the drawn
curtain!

È UNA SONERIA costante; un micidiale compromettersi
una didascalia infruttuosa, e un vento di traverso
mentre battendo le ciglia sentenziavo una
saggezza imbrogliata.

Conto di farla finita con le forme, i loro
bisbigliamenti, i loro contenuti contenenti
tutta la urgente scatola della mia anima la
quale indifferente al problema farebbe meglio
a contenersi. Giocattoli sono le strade e
infermiere sono le abitudini distrutte da
un malessere generale.

La gola nella montagna si offrì pulita al
mio desiderio di continuare la menzogna indecifrabile
come le sigarette che fumo.

IT RINGS CONSTANTLY; a deadly compromise
a fruitless caption, and a crosswind
while blinking I proclaimed an
embroiled wisdom.

I expect to end it with forms, their
whispers, their contents containing
the whole urgent box of my soul which
indifferent to the problem would do better
to contain itself. Toys are the streets and
nurses are habits destroyed by
a general malaise.

The mountain's gorge offered itself cleansed to
my desire to continue the indecipherable lie
like the cigarettes I smoke.

FORTE NELLA SUA tubercolosità
ministeriale nella sua carcassa
(carcassa surgelata)
come se fossero
intelligenti animali
beffeggiando e rivalutando
incorso nella paura di morire d'inedia
nell'ultima stanza
un pollo pronto per la miscela
le amarezze
attentamente finsero
oltre il midollo della carne che parla,
e si silenzia

muore nell'ottobrino
il candore delle tue parole illuminate.

Strong in its ministerial
tuberculosity in its carcass
(frozen carcass)
as if they were
intelligent animals

mocking and re-evaluating
a chicken ready for the mixture
faced the fear of dying of starvation
in the last room
bitterness
carefully pretended
beyond the marrow of the speaking flesh,
and it falls silent

dies octoberish
the candor of your enlightened words.

L'IMMAGINAZIONE TORTURATA SI tormentava
gli idilli nascevano e si tramutavano
in fantascientifico dubbio o nausea
e l'amore era un gioco di scacchi.

Il fantasma che regnava nella casa vuota
il fiero dedicarsi ai combattimenti
tutto prendeva una piega imprevista
se il dolor di capo ricominciava.

È nel voler dar fiducia e nel dover
toglierla, il perpetuo scacco della
regina: non ha fiducia, né può darla
mentre i lustrascarpe s'industriano.

Gli alberi assassini s'accovacciano,
foglie libere e deliberate hanno conti
aperti col vento; e l'ira della regina
si tramuta in angoscia col vento!

Il vento stesso si tramuta in libidine
col vento!

THE TORTURED IMAGINATION tormented itself
idylls were born and were transformed
into science fiction doubt or nausea
and love was a game of chess.

The ghost reigning in the empty house
the proud dedication to fighting
everything took an unexpected turn
if the headache returned.

It's in wanting to trust and in having to
cast trust aside, the perpetual check to the
queen: she lacks trust, nor can she bestow it
while shoe shiners get by.

The killer trees crouch,
leaves at liberty and deliberate have a score
to settle with the wind; and the queen's wrath
turns into anguish with the wind!

The wind itself turns into lust
with the wind!

IN UNA CAMERA d'albergo, a meditare
il peggio, un angelo
cogitava il meglio.
Corrompersi e poi portare al ritrovo
tutta quella canaglia!

E io ritrovo, nel
ritornare a casa, qualcosa di dimenticato:
il peggio di me stessa. Oh
stancata dedizione a quei particolari
che non hanno presa sul mondo!
nei particolari l'orrore svaporato.

Stordirsi: comprensivi.
E tanti umori a fertilizzare questo vuoto...

Ho vuota stanchezza:
la sua terra non era mia quando per prima
la fertilizzai, tra
tante realtà. Oh mia realtà scappata
nel bosco! e nelle loro nere
automobili le preoccupazioni sembravano
sbirciare.

La paura, sottile pugnale,
oh che contenti sono i galli
la mia magrezza
non può darsi all'alba.

Quel biscotto sotto
le ruote del treno,
l'amaro corpo
spirito disorientato.

IN A HOTEL room, meditating upon
the worst, an angel
cogitated the best.
Corrupt yourself and then take that utter
rogue to the hideout!

And I take up, upon
returning home, something forgotten:
the worst of myself. Oh
tired dedication to those details
lacking a grip on the world!
in the details the evaporated horror.

Stunning yourself: sympathetic.
And so many humors to fertilize this void...

My void fatigue:
this land wasn't mine when I first
fertilized it, among
many realities. Oh my reality ran off
to the woods! and worries
seemed to peek out from their
black cars.

Fear, thin dagger,
oh how happy are the roosters
my thinness
cannot exist at dawn.

That wafer below
the wheels of the train,
the bitter body
disoriented spirit.

Hai venduto la mia vita
la secca prudenza
in te dei rivali leziosi, scorribande –
pensieri ben più facinorosi,

prima volli sapere da lui perché l'uomo
ha tanto condono in sé.

You sold my life
the dry prudence
in you simpering rivals, raids—
thoughts far more troublesome,

first I wanted to know from him why man
condones so much.

QUESTO GIOCO
in altri perplesso e soffocato:
è aria compressa
è psiche compressa,
si vanta di adoperarlo.

Muta e in soggezione rincorro il vuoto
non finisco il mio gioco,
nella contentezza del domani

pur di slittare
tra le grandi vie del quinto piano,
tra i solipsismi della primavera
questo scempio
o sciame di api.

THIS GAME
in others perplexed and suffocated:
it's compressed air
it's compressed psyche,
she boasts of using it.

Mute and in awe I chase the void
I don't finish my game,
in the happiness of tomorrow

just to sled
down the wide streets of the fifth floor,
down the solipsisms of spring
this mess
or swarm of bees.

Questo odio nelle facce altrui
dita fini intrecciate
in segno di buona volontà
turgida liturgia
oggetto
di alcune sue riflessioni
fuoco divampa nel cerchio inflessibile
come sbarazzarsi della realtà
abolendo ogni riserva ma è
solo l'anima in pena che si descrive
mentre paradossalmente non si prescrive
altro che accomodamenti.

Seccamente è pronta
non per scelta ma per circostanza.

THIS HATE IN others' faces
slim interlaced fingers
as a sign of good will
turgid liturgy
object
of some of her reflections
fire blazes in the inflexible circle
how to get rid of reality
abolishing every reservation for it's
only the lost soul describing itself
while paradoxically not prescribing itself
other than accommodation.

Dryly she's ready
not by choice but by circumstance.

Lettera

Vento da galeotti stasera e tutta la
radura rade il mio cuore e l'osmosi
del bene e del male vien trattenuta

da un irresistibile bisogno di pianto,
da lucertole divine fra i semi della

rivolta: che non avviene, e nemmeno
le lucertole viaggiano per il tuo cuore!

se con la smania appariscente di apparire
vogliamo galoppare per i prati smorti
dell'intendimento di versi a noi ignoti

la luna relegata in un letto di morti
e il canto a noi noto dei morti: questi

versi che salgono scalinando per impervie
vie del tramonto, non taciono.

Letter

Gallows wind tonight and all the
clearing clears my heart and the osmosis
of good and evil is withheld

by an irresistible urge to cry,
by divine lizards among the seeds of

revolt: that doesn't happen, nor do
the lizards travel through your heart!

if with showy frenzy to show up
we want to gallop through the dull meadows
of the meaning of lines unknown to us

the moon relegated to a bed of deaths
and the song of the dead known to us: these

climbing lines climbing impervious
sunset lanes, unhushed.

FERMI A UN destino sempre semovente
o irriconoscibile tra gli alti pini
stentati, tra le tante altre cose
di cui non scriviamo purché riusciamo
a viverle, fra le tende del camping
v'erano infatti i soliti traditori:
me stessa travisata da imperatore povero
che mi guadagnavo a fatica un posto
dove vivere. Ho disfatto tutti i tunnel
della contr'ora: felicità di potersi scambiare
dure parole o felicità di potersi annullare
nel dolore di pochi che unisce
i molti, virtù nascosta e dolce
a chi scrive di cose indescrivibili.

STILL BEFORE A destiny ever self-moving
or unrecognizable among the tall stunted
pines, among many other things
of which we don't write as long as we succeed
in living them, among the tents of the campsite
there were in fact the usual traitors:
myself misread as a poor emperor
barely earning a place
to live. I unpacked all the tunnels
of midday lull: happiness of exchanging
harsh words or happiness of withdrawing
in the pain of the few that unites
the many, virtue hidden and sweet
for those who write of indescribable things.

ASCOLTA
la furia dei venti contrari –
ho contato gli alibi
i conti correnti postali
striduli pittori pornografici
lo sfracellamento
dell'eleganza.

Cielo bagnato,
false statue
nei giardini.

Listen
to the fury of the headwinds—
I counted alibis
postal accounts
shrill pornographic painters
the smashing
of elegance.

Wet sky,
false statues
in the gardens.

CONVERSAZIONI MOLTO SFATICATE
hanno radicato in me la voglia
di cantare la svogliatezza
in un momento d'abbandono
o di disperazione.

Confondendo l'ingegno a bella
posta tirai via per le lunghe
una conversazione tutta fatta
di abboccamenti e di velleità

pur di salvare in qualche
modo la verità.

Poi vidi anche luccicare tra
le pareti ben protette da
un loro osservarsi beffardamente
quel che non osavo chiamare

per il suo vero nome: il nulla
divenuto però incandescente
e separato dal vostro vivere

ostile come i loro ammiccamenti
le loro amicizie per lo spazio
che ci protegge inconsapevole

più che non tutta la nostra
benevolenza per i martoriati
e i loro stipendiati.

SUCH INDOLENT CONVERSATIONS
have rooted in me the wish
to sing listlessness
in a moment of abandonment
or despair.

Confusing ingenuity on purpose
I dragged it out
a conversation put together
of encounters and wishful thinking

just to attempt somehow to save
the truth.

Then I saw as well a shimmering
between well-protected walls from
their mocking self-scrutiny
what I didn't dare call

by its real name: nothingness
become instead incandescent
and separated from your hostile

living like their winks
their friendships in the space
that unwittingly protects us

more than all our
good will for the battered ones
and their salaried.

SIAMO NELLA VERDE ombra del deserto
e vivi sempre assieme a tuo fratello
corrosa da nessuna attitudine.

Linguaggio divenuto senile abitudine
feconda intelligenza col nemico
frase impercettibile nel silenzio
il suo acume di uomo doloroso.

Un sole bianchissimo di faccia alle
finestre spazza via quel resto di
programma programmandone altri che
però non hanno quel noioso rigore

di cose in cui non credi.

WE'RE IN THE desert's green shadow
and you still live with your brother
untainted by any inclination.

Language becomes senile disposition
fertile intelligence with the enemy
inaudible sentence in the silence
the acumen of a painful man.

A whitest sun facing the
windows wipes out the rest of
the program by programming others
but they lack that boring rigor

of things you don't believe in.

UN FOGLIO VERDE o arancione non
ho mai capito bene cosa ci stavi
a fare là dietro all'albereto.

Ma più tardi era già tardi a quell'ora
per capirci meglio e così indagare
sull'origine dei nostri ardori

o dei nostri livori. È così scarsa
la gioventù di baci che penso proprio
sia fatta piuttosto per odiare.

Risplendevi: e ti rincorrevo, per
poi distruggerti per vendetta, non
volendo capitolare.

E se ti dicessi che non a me appartiene
il giudicarti? – fuggiresti via
più stranito di prima.

Prima eri un re e ora sei un arancio
malinconico chi lo tocca.

A GREEN OR orange piece of paper I
never quite understood what you were
doing back there behind the arboretum.

But later it was already too late at that hour
to get to understand each other better and
then explore the origin of our ardor

or our rancor. Youth is so
stingy with kisses that I rather think
it's really made to hate.

You shone: and I chased you, only
to destroy you in revenge, not
wanting to capitulate.

What if I told you it's not for me
to judge you?—you'd run away
more dazed than before.

At first a king now you're an orange tree
melancholic whoever touches it.

MENTRE CON LA testa in fiamme
ricerchi altre spiagge ben
men deserte che non questa
fatica di essere, con me tu
non sei se non te stesso: quale
non vuoi essere.

WHILE WITH YOUR head on fire
you look for other beaches much
less deserted than this
malaise ever is, with me you're
nothing but yourself: which
you don't want to be.

Uccelli gradevoli sui tetti spioventi
l'acqua s'infiltra tra
le rotte case
malessere sincero
la bottiglia là galoppa su
un tavolo di legno rozzo,
questa tua infanzia rattristata
severa o diabolica.

Cucine luccicanti
piangere su questo fazzoletto rosso,
tua meritevole risposta:
mi travolse quel bisogno
di contemplarti che non tutti conoscono
quando cercano la gloria.

Quando cercano la gloria ritrovano la
gloria e quando cercano la morte ritrovano
poi la vita.

Inclined birds on the sloped roofs
water seeps in between
the broken houses
true malaise
the bottle gallops over there
across a rough wooden table,
your saddened childhood
harsh or diabolical.

Sparkling kitchens
crying into this red handkerchief,
your worthy reply:
that need sweeping over me
to contemplate you unknown to many
who seek glory.

When they seek glory they find
glory and when they seek death they
find life.

CONATI DI LIBERTÀ splendida e vuota
un cerchio un poco troppo vuoto
centro splendido e vuoto
nelle

loro vacue splendide tristi abitabili
ville

e nel vino v'era anche
una grossa intuizione: la gioventù

mentre infilando un panino
ti sconquassavo volentieri nelle risaie.

Efforts of splendid and empty freedom
a circle a little too empty
splendid and empty center
in

their vacuous splendid sad habitable
villas

and in the wine there was also
a great intuition: youth

while loading a sandwich
I'd gladly crack you up in the rice paddies.

GELOSA DELLO SPAZIO che ti contiene
preclude, consuma, e lontana da te come
per negativo miracolo il sopruso della
vita riappare
e ricordarmi le sue vere usanze.

Volendo
tenere in vita quello che non osa morire
travasata dalle stelle stesse
toccava la di lor carne.

Scostare la
carne, no
non toccate il di me grembo.

Veramente risposero le stelle primarie
io riconosco che il vuoto
è quello che mai avrei voluto o supposto
di me stessa.

Il vivo vuoto è questo inordinato
credersi superiori alla norma!

JEALOUS OF THE space precluding,
consuming, holding you, and far from you
as if by a negative miracle the abuse of
life reappears
and reminds me of its true mores.

Wanting
to keep alive what doesn't dare to die
poured from the stars themselves
she touched that flesh of theirs.

Moving the flesh
aside, no
don't touch this womb of mine.

Indeed the primary stars answered
I recognize that void
is what I never wanted or supposed
of myself.

The vital void is this inordinate
believing yourself above the norm!

MIO ANGELO, IO non seppi mai quale angelo
fosti, o per quali vie storte ti amai
o venerai, tu che scendendo ogni gradino
sembravi salirli, frustarmi, mostrarmi
una via tutta perduta alla ragione, quando
facesti al caso quel che esso riprometteva,
cioè mi lasciasti.

Non seppi nemmeno perché tra tanti chiarori
eccitati dell'intelletto in pena, vi
furono così sotterranee evoluzioni d'un
accordarsi al mio, al vostro e tuo bisogno
d'una sterilità completa.

Eppure eccomi qua, a scrivere versi,
come se fosse non del tutto astratto
alla mia ricerca d'un enciclopedico
capire quasi tutto a me offerto senza
lo spazio d'una volontà di ferro a controllare
quel poco del tutto così mal offerto.

My angel, I never knew which angel
you were, or for which crooked ways I loved you
or worshipped you, you who descending each step
seemed to climb them, whipping me, showing me
a path fully lost to reason, when
you did what was meant to be,
that is you left.

I didn't even know why among so much elated
glinting of the afflicted intellect, there
were so many underground evolutions
attuned to my need, and yours
for a complete sterility.

And yet here I am, writing verses,
as if it weren't completely abstracted
from my search for an encyclopedic
understanding, most of it offered to me without
the space of an iron will to control
that little of everything so poorly offered.

Lo SDRUCCIOLO CUORE che in me è ribelle
quasi sempre in me preferirebbe
una più saggia angoscia
l'animo è davvero poca cosa
è davvero
infernale così come tu dici.

Ma credevo nel soldo e nella miseria
assieme assetati di vendetta: o credevo
nel lento pellegrinaggio ad una fonte
dedicata ad un pubblico e anche privatissimo
dibattito, che essa ingigantisce
così ingegnosa.

Nessuna fede ha mai mosso le montagne
tu muovi le montagne in me, tu che sei
compagno di un momento e senza amore
con quel tuo chiarore di corta vita
l'estate stessa spiovente
nel suo abracadabra di giovinezza irresponsabile
ricevo dalle tue abbondanti e magrissime
braccia.

THE SLIPPERY HEART so rebellious in me
for all of me it would almost always prefer
a wiser anguish
the soul isn't really much at all
it's really
infernal as you say.

But I believed in money and poverty
thirsting together for revenge: or I believed
in the slow pilgrimage to a spring
dedicated to a public and also very private
debate, which it magnifies
so ingeniously.

No faith has ever moved mountains
you move mountains in me, you who are
companion of a moment and loveless
with that brief life glint of yours
sloped summer itself
in its abracadabra of irresponsible youth
I receive from your abundant and skinniest
arms.

SENZA DI TE
trafitto, io non so disgiungere la conoscenza
dall'aborto ferraceo
(come d'un candido lettino infantile
separato).

Poi ho ritrovato una luce
intatta, che era una sorta di paradiso
mal digerito.

Un paio d'occhi celesti incerti,
un sogno o due,
giù per la pineta maleodorante:
non seppi più
credere alla realtà con certezza guidandola
per meno amorosi boschi.

WITHOUT YOU
pierced, I don't know how to sever knowledge
from an iron abortion
(like a child's snow-white
cot).

Then I found an intact
light, a poorly digested
kind of paradise.

A pair of uncertain blue eyes,
a dream or two,
down the rank pine forest:
I could no longer
believe in reality guiding it with certainty
through less loving woods.

STERCO DI ANIMALE robusto ha
sedotto la mia anima robusta ma venata
di fallace o forte malinconia.

Luci attente attirano a sé i sogni per
poi scacciarli distrattamente
robuste anch'esse
come un finto, fertile ma astratto
incontro.

La plastica era robusta
artificiosa, impossibile
e il tuo bacio quasi
furioso.

Robust animal dung has
seduced my soul robust yet veined
with strong or fallacious melancholy.

Attentive lights attract dreams
then drive them away distractedly
robust too
like a feigned, fertile but abstract
encounter.

Plastic was robust
artificial, impossible
and your kiss almost
furious.

VITTORIOSI D'UN NULLA sul nulla, la
camera si risvegliò latente
il freddo tagliente,
quell'inferno che fu inverno
s'abbandonò, al muro
nel suo piccolo violetto raggio violetto
finto corsetto,
dei poveri e dei loro voti,
povero di sé e di se stessi.

Lago artificiale gettato lì per caso
di tra fiori chiusi, le
finestre scabrose,
nel loro fermaglio assurdo di volontà
la poesia obbedì
al dolore istintivo degli adulti,
come fosse
che nella festa sincronizzata
ci passassimo il pane da una mano all'altra
il verso battendo la sua strada consueta
imperdonabile, supplicando furbesco.

La sua casa bianca d'un grigio
pertinente, fissandola negli occhi
gli apparve quel muro disinfetto
e quasi perfetto,
inventato
da te e per te
di questa inversione d'un ordine
garantito risuonando
in quella stanza il passo vuoto del
paesaggio di sasso, la vernice appositamente.

VICTORIOUS IN NOTHING over nothing, the
room covert awoke
the biting cold,
that hell of a winter
abandoned itself, to the wall
with its small violet violet ray
fake corset,
of the poor and their vows,
poor in itself and in themselves.

Artificial lake cast there by chance
between closed flowers,
rough windows,
with their absurd clasp of will
poetry obeyed
the instinctive pain of adults,
how it was
that at the synchronized party
we passed the bread from hand to hand
the line wending its usual way
unforgivable, pleading cunningly.

His white house of a pertinent
gray, staring into her eyes
that wall appeared to him disinfected
and almost perfected,
invented
by you and for you
in this reversal of a guaranteed
order resounding
in that room the empty step of the
stone landscape, painted expressly.

PUNTANDO LE DITA sul terriccio
ogni giorno fissamente guardando
morte del fiore nel giardino trepidante
impossibile o possibile semplicità
come una qualsiasi rara bestia
ogni giorno nella mia esistenza scrivendoti
tu non eri pensieroso
povera bestia di una lettera
tutte le frivolezze riscontrabili
nel mio turbolento deporre le tristezze
tu canonizzato oramai.

Vive, s'ammazza ogni giorno
finché il suo pensiero si fa misantropico
poi si spara nell'ombra
sapendo d'essere esente
coi suoi speciali occhiali color castano.

Poi dedicata ad un nulla fastidioso
e vi trovai soltanto carta straccia:
tu mi disubbidisci lentamente
illustrando ogni pagina
fu quel mio suicidarmi distrattamente
nel tuo silenzio antropomorfo
una tua tasca aperta gonfia.

In quella pineta c'eri
e gli altri pallidi veloci
e non riscontrabili nel tornaconto
del giardino di una malavita pensierosa.

Il maschio vestito di nero o era lutto
s'impiccò al chiodo infisso

POINTING FINGERS AT the soil
every day staring fixedly
the flower's death in the expectant garden
impossible or possible simplicity
like any rare beast
every day of my life writing to you
you weren't pensive
poor beast of a letter
all verifiable frivolities
in my turbulent setting aside of sorrows
you're canonized by now.

She lives, kills herself daily
until her thought turns misanthropic
then she shoots herself in the shadow
sentient of being exempt
with her special brown eyeglasses.

Then dedicated to an irritating nothing
in which I found only wastepaper:
you disobey me slowly
illustrating each page
it was my absent-minded suicide
in your anthropomorphic silence
your swollen open pocket.

You were in that pine forest
and the others pallid swift
and unverifiable in the profit
of a pensive underworld garden.

The male dressed in black or in mourning
hanged himself on the fixed nail

sarà d'aiuto alle vacanti generazioni
ritrovato adagiato
nel taglio d'un muro o di un quadro
maschio bastante.

he'll be of help to the vacant generations
found lying down
in the cut of a wall or of a picture
male enough.

FOSSE STATO PIÙ facile spartirti,
nella quiete impazzita o pomeridiana...

ed ora costruisco ponti inavvertiti
le mie pantofole trattenute nell'armadio
gli altri che m'inflatano
quella luna così cara
scansarsi inequivocabilmente!

La luna-boom, il mio danaro...

HAD IT BEEN easier sharing you,
in the crazed or afternoon quiet...

and now I build unseen bridges
my slippers retained in the closet
the others inflating me
that moon so dear
dodging unequivocally!

The moon-boom, my money...

È FIAMMA DI volontà
mia stupida fede
sicura come una tomba,
questo sordo
lottare delle «ore tristi».

Vetrata quella chiesa:
la stingeremo,
tingeremo di proprietà precise: «come
salvarsi l'anima», prima che nevicasse un

nulla ben più rischioso, prezioso.

It's a flame of will
my foolish faith
safe as a tomb,
this deaf
struggling of the "sad hours."

Glassy that church:
we'll dim it,
we'll dye it with precise properties: "how to
save your soul," before it snowed

nothing riskier, more precious.

LA TUA FACCIA indelebile sulla carta
se non fosse che tu esisti o esiti
fuori d'ogni consistenza
del piacere.

Hai finito per distrarmi dalla realtà
che seguo con finti e volitivi passi
tutta una storia luminosa di tamponamenti
con la mia lealtà ad un'immagine attentamente
classificata
ad assembrarne diligentemente i resti.

Assordante colpa
non ho ancora contato le estati passate
a ripetere sempre lo stesso gesto
che eri tu mia colpa preferita per
desiderio d'un fine più sublime.
Verità fuori usanza nelle mie contrade,
vicinissime contrade voi sembrate ripetere
lo stesso turbinìo di pensieri
questo nostro essere prostrati dall'indicibile
indefinito tuo premere per ottenere

stanza d'albergo severa e vuota.

Your indelible face on paper
if it weren't that you exist or hesitate
beyond every consistency
of pleasure.

You ended up distracting me from the reality
I follow with feigned and willful steps
the whole luminous history of collisions
with my loyalty to an image so carefully
classified
as to diligently assemble the remains.

Deafening guilt
I've yet to count summers spent
forever repeating the same gesture
that it was you my preferred guilt for
desiring a more sublime end.
Truth outmoded in my quarters,
closest quarters you seem to repeat
the same whirl of thoughts
our being crushed by your unspeakable
undefined pressure to obtain

a stark and empty hotel room.

NON QUESTO SUPPLIZIO
mitigato dall'intelligenza
questo spartirti
in tanti piccoli pezzi.

Cosa facevi lì sul tuo albereto, cosa
facevo io su quel mio prugno,
tutto questo trambusto del mio cuore
la tirannia aperta al
dubbio.

Ne colpì l'immagine vetrata
con pugni arcigni nel
sottile muro per sempre.

NOT THIS TORTURE
mitigated by intelligence
this sharing of yourself
in so many small pieces.

What were you doing atop your arboretum, what
was I doing on that plum tree,
all this turmoil of my heart
tyranny open to
doubt.

With grim fists she struck
the glassy image
on the thin wall forever.

IL PORTANOME DI questa lettera bizzarra
sembra scappare all'aprire dell'aurora
invidio i maestri di botanica,
la letteratura paragonata ad un batticuore.

Stringenti alibi, la moltitudine
delle facce zittisce l'inferiore
o infernale faccia del mondo:

vento nordico
parlando pazzescamente tra le cipolle
perle nella bocca dimagrita
in crudo marmo fedelmente:

un impazzimento serio o serioso
nel vuoto della mia spenta giovinezza
pruneto grande come la mia immaginazione
per qualche giorno tra spaventati passi
non è detto ch'io sia

poi questo labirintico salire e scendere
d'energia.

THE NAME BEARER of this bizarre letter
seems to escape at the aurora of dawn
I envy botany masters,
literature likened to a beating heart.

Stringent alibis, the multitude
of faces silences the inferior
or infernal face of the world:

northerly wind
speaking madly among the onions
pearls in the thin mouth
faithful in raw marble:

a serious or most serious madness
in the void of my spent youth
plum bush big as my imagination
for a few days amid frightened strides
it doesn't mean that I'm

this labyrinthine rise and fall
of energy.

LA PASSIONE MI divorò giustamente
la passione mi divise fortemente
la passione mi ricondusse saggiamente
io saggiamente mi ricondussi

alla passione saggistica, principiante
nell'oscuro bosco d'un noioso
dovere, e la passione che bruciava

nel sedere a tavola con i grandi
senza passione o volendola dimenticare

io che bruciavo di passione
estinta la passione nel bruciare

io che bruciavo di dolore, nel
vedere la passione così estinta.
Estinguere la passione bramosa!
Distinguere la passione dal

vero bramare la passione estinta
estinguere tutto quel che è

estinguere tutto ciò che rima
con è: estinguere me, la passione
la passione fortemente bruciante
che si estinse da sé.

Estinguere la passione del sé!
estinguere il verso che rima
da sé: estinguere perfino me

PASSION RIGHTLY DEVOURED me
passion strongly divided me
passion sagely brought me back
I sagely brought myself back

to the passion of the sage, beginner
in the dark wood of a boring
duty, and passion that burned

sitting at the table with the grown-ups
without passion or wanting to forget it

I, burning with passion
passion burned to extinction

I, burning with pain, seeing
passion thus go extinct.
Extinguishing greedy passion!
Distinguishing passion from the

real greed for the extinct passion
extinguishing all that could be

extinguishing everything that rhymes
with be: extinguishing me, passion
the passion burning strongly
extinguished by itself.

Extinguishing the passion of the self!
extinguishing the verse that rhymes
by itself: extinguishing even myself

estinguere tutte le rime in
«e»: forse vinse la passione
estinguendo la rima in «e».

extinguishing all the rhymes in
"be:" maybe passion won
by extinguishing the rhyme in "be."

PROPONGO UN INCONTRO col teschio,
una sfida al teschio
mantengo ferma e costante
chiusa nella fede impossibile
l'amore proprio
delle bestie.

Ogni giorno della sua inesplicabile esistenza
parole mute in fila.

I PROPOSE AN encounter with the skull,
a challenge to the skull
I maintain firm and constant
locked in impossible faith
the amour propre
of beasts.

Every day of its inexplicable existence
mute words lined up.

UNA VOLTA RAGGIUNTO lo scopo
piccolo albergo nel mio cielo candido
splendido sole inutilizzato
questa nostra vita che rabbrividisce
d'uno sgomento preso a prestito

se lui non corre abbastanza io gareggio.

Once the goal is achieved
little refuge in my candid sky
splendid unused sun
our life shivering
with borrowed dismay

if he doesn't speed up I'll compete.

STONA LA VITA,
si spegne da sé
la speranza si spiuma
faticosa a mettersi insieme non
ne vuol più sapere

i pensieri sono poi ovali, o opachi.

OUT OF TUNE life,
it blows itself out
hope is plucked
hard to piece itself together
wants nothing to do with it

thoughts are oval then, or opaque.

I CANALI LINFATICI odorosi
di zanzare
nella baracca vuota
ormai nessuno può più metter mano
nodose storie
scambiandole per una metafora.

LYMPHATIC CANALS SCENTED
with mosquitoes
in the empty shack
now no one can ever lay a hand
knotted stories
mistaking them for a metaphor.

ALIBI A FORMA di ventaglio
una cavalleria del cuore
dormire su questi lauri
con l'arena
d'uno sgradevole pallore.

La pace l'ho persa
sporgendo denunzia al vuoto.

Miscreduto
solo col rospo s'affaccia
ad un'operetta del buon senso.

Fan-shaped alibis
a cavalry of the heart
resting on these laurels
the arena
of an unpleasant pallor.

I lost peace
pleading with the void.

Misbelieved
alone with the toad looking out
at an operetta of common sense.

Campagnano Paese

Silenzi aborigeni; pasta all'uovo, se
poi sono così svelta da separare la

terra dal bene astratto così velocemente
rinnegato.

Campagnano

Aboriginal silences; egg pasta, if
only I'm quick enough to separate the

ground from the abstract good so speedily
denied.

Ho distolto ogni luce
sdrammatizzo la tua primavera
lui che si pettina.

Quel terreno indifferente
e tu dove sei,
che nascevi con la scienza.

Vedendomi scritta sui muri
varcai l'isolotto.

I've removed each light
downplayed your spring
his combing his hair.

That indifferent land
and where are you,
born with science.

Seeing myself written on the walls
I crossed the islet.

Genuine genuflessioni – una rivalità

vincendovi con un riottoso sorriso, solidamente priva di senso.

GENUINE GENUFLECTIONS—A RIVALRY

winning you with a riotous grin, consistently meaningless.

RIPOSO IL CAPO
sulla tua cappa
carta d'interesse sfoderata.

Perfin la vita fece voltare
la faccia al muro
me la distruggesti
se non distruggere almeno fiaccare
nello sbadiglio o nel bagaglio
assembraggio di piuttosto
voci che sentimento.

Forte appetito come il
mio, più tentennante
che non questo tuo «te»
nel mentre il mondo
intero trainava questo nostro
mito d'una rivalità placata.

Amore a piene mani:
erano perfetti,
il destino gettava la spugna.

I rest my pate
on your cape
unsheathed interest card.

Even life made
the wall turn face
you destroyed it for me
if not destroyed at least played out
in the yawn or in the carry on
the assembling of voices
rather than feelings.

A good appetite like
mine, more burbling
than your bumbling
while the whole
world hauled our
myth of an appeased rivalry.

Love with both hands:
they were perfect,
fate threw in the towel.

NESSUNO
ammise d'esser stato tradito
finsi calma frenavo il pianto
poi riportando il dato in
cronaca.

Stanando periodici dal loro
comodo cassetto,
il pavimento costretto a
spianarsi.

Sminuito impero,
non era sicuro di poter tentare il tragitto
passato il tempo in cui nello *slip*
ti guardavi contenta, accontentata
d'un umore qualsiasi
follie-bergères dietro ogni
mobile, spostabile definitivamente
ogni mattina.

Gli si chiedeva l'artifizio
la nona sinfonia, l'estratto
coniugale stretto tra due pugni:
un nervosismo
forse una angolazione
sbadata:

come la promiscuità.

NOBODY
admitted having been betrayed
I pretended to be calm stopped crying
then reported the fact in
the news.

Digging out magazines from their
handy drawer,
the flooring forced to
level itself.

Diminished empire,
he wasn't sure he could attempt the jaunt
past the time in which you contentedly
looked in your panties, contented
with whatever mood
follies-bergères behind each
piece of furniture, permanently moveable
each morning.

He was asked the artifice
the ninth symphony, the marital
extract tight between two fists:
a nervousness
maybe a heedless
angle:

like promiscuity.

NELLA SOLA IMMAGINAZIONE
a farmi vedere il bene che era
tu (che ordinasti il cattivo tempo)
fosti l'apogeo delle cattive notti
possidente d'un sogno
ribaltabile
mia tenerezza dai posti vacanti.

Tu, verde collina senza orizzonte
fosti tu non possibile
spaesata percorrevi
le tue linee diritte –
il cuore divenne fegato,
erano mercato assiduo.

L'oceano si fece:
il collo in posizione
difficilissima.

IN IMAGINATION ALONE
to show me the good that was,
you (who ordered the bad weather)
were the apogee of bad nights
owner of a capsized
dream
my tenderness of vacant places.

You, horizonless green hill
were you not possible
lost along the path
of your straight lines—
the heart became the liver,
they were an assiduous market.

The ocean became:
the neck in a most awkward
position.

QUEL MATTINO DOPO segretamente
all'impresario ogni conto
non le mie mani ma le vostre

THAT MORNING AFTER secretly
to the contractor every account
not my hands but yours

Così nel furore lanciatissima
datemi i complotti semplici
voi tutti nemici e tecnici
pulire i pavimenti altrui
di commovente periferia
lottando con la periferia
ma la profondità annoia.

Ma son io ma voi in cima
queste scale così gemelle
fuori posto quel giorno
alto il bisogno di gloria
bisogna ch'io metta i piedi.

Suora facile che saremo
giorno dal pallido tramonto
guarda la luna e soddisfati
la carne è come il gatto
simbolo sessuale in piena.

Piace ch'io faccia questo
lui pericolosamente s'addentrava
(povera suora)
imperniare il discorso sulle
rare qualità, in versione
letteraria o no.

SO FURIOUSLY WILD
give me simple plots
all of you enemies and engineers
cleaning the floors of others
of affecting peripheries
struggling with the peripheries
but depth bores.

But it's me but it's you at the top
these stairs so twinned
out of place that day
strong need for glory
I need to set my feet.

Easy nun we'll be
day by the pale sunset
look at the moon and be satisfied
flesh is like a cat
sexual symbol in flood.

They like that I do this
he dangerously entered
(poor nun)
focusing on
rare qualities, in literary
form or not.

C'È COME UN dolore nella stanza, ed
è superato in parte: ma vince il peso
degli oggetti, il loro significare
peso e perdita.

C'è come un rosso nell'albero, ma è
l'arancione della base della lampada
comprata in luoghi che non voglio ricordare
perché anch'essi pesano.

Come nulla posso sapere della tua fame
precise nel volere
sono le stilizzate fontane
può ben situarsi un rovescio d'un destino
di uomini separati per obliquo rumore.

THERE'S SOMETHING LIKE pain in the room, and
it's partly over: but the weight of objects
wins, their meaning
weight and loss.

There's something like red in the tree, but it's
the orange of the base of the lamp
bought in places I don't want to remember
because they too weigh.

How can I know anything of your hunger
the stylized fountains
are precise in their will
it may well be the reversal of the destiny
of men separated by oblique noise.

Nuvoli a ritroso,
sistemati in un campo verde
posso soltanto immaginarti scritto
fluttuante d'angosce o ritardi
questo ritmo benpensante
cosa fare se poi
rifiuta di adorarti.

Backwards clouds
arranged in a green field
I can only imagine you written
fluctuating with anxiety or delays
this right-minded rhythm
what to do if then it
refuses to worship you.

NEL SELCIATO UGUALE
laconici biglietti al muro
doloroso giuoco nell'istigarmi
ad una specie di pace senza rivoltella
degli alberi piantati lì apposta
col loro rivedermi lì in quel lusso
nessuna ragione impedendomi di
vederli poi anche loro aggrapparsi
così penetrabili.

Invero vero che tu non m'ami.

ON THE SAME pavement
laconic notes on the wall
painful game of inciting me
to a kind of peace without a revolver
trees planted there on purpose
their seeing me back there in that luxury
nothing preventing me from
then seeing them clinging too
so penetrable.

Truth truly that you don't love me.

Sciopero generale 1969

lampade accesissime e nell'urlo
d'una quieta folla rocambolesca
trovarsi lì a far sul serio: cioè
rischiare! che nell'infantilismo
apparente schianti anche il mio
potere d'infischiarmene.

Un Dio molto interno poteva bastare
non bastò a me il mio egoismo

non bastò a queste genti il sapore
d'una ricchezza nella rivincita

del resto strozzata. Dovevamo
esprimere il meglio: regalarsi

ad una retorica che era urlo
di protesta ad una distruzione

impavida nelle nostre impaurite
case. (Persi da me quell'amore
al verticale, a solitario dio
rivoluzionandomi nella gente
asportandomi dal cielo.)

General Strike 1969

brightest lamps and in the howl
of a quiet rambunctious crowd
to be there and take it seriously: that is
to risk! may in the apparent
childishness crash even my
power of not giving a damn.

An innermost God could be enough
my selfishness wasn't enough for me

wasn't enough for these people
the taste of riches in a choked

revenge after all. We had to
express the best: treat yourself

to a rhetoric that was a howl
of protest at a fearless

destruction in our frightened
homes. (I lost it myself that
vertical love, a solitary god
revolutionizing myself in people
removing myself from the sky.)

Rosa ripulita
solitudine dimenticabile
contadino meticoloso
migliore del mondo
riconoscersi serbatoio
di nullità recondita
sfinita sopraffazione
morte-solitudine
tanto più pregevole
se sottile m'armo.

Rose tidied up
forgettable loneliness
meticulous farmer
best in the world
recognizing yourself as a tank
of covert nullity
spent crushing
death-solitude
all the more valuable
if thinly I'm marble.

LE TUE MANI bianche
le querele dei poveri perdonando
o forzando le querele
suono campane mute.

YOUR WHITE HANDS
forgiving complaints of the poor
or forcing complaints
I play mute bells.

FIUMI IN LACRIME stanchissime
se, nell'inverno odoroso
di valide piogge, lasciandosi
incantare o incatenare, si
sparge la voce del tuo rimorso.

Questi temporaleschi bisogni
questi nastri d'ottone!
Ho riso del mio defunto
destino, destinatario d'ogni
perdono o rivoluzione.

E silenzio riscopre l'orario
la lava del fornello è spenta
delicata la menomazione
la figurazione degli angioli.

Imperfetti sono gli angioli
eri di legno, eri di legno
imbracciare allora quel quadro
tappezzato il cervello di grigio.

Rivers in weariest tears
if, in the winter scented
with valid rains, enchanted
or enchained, word
spreads of your remorse.

These thunderous needs
these brass strips!
I laughed at my defunct
destiny, destination of every
forgiveness or revolution.

And silence uncovers the hours
spent lava from the burner
delicate diminution
figuration of angels.

Angels are imperfect
you were wooden, you were wooden
holding that picture then
the brain wallpapered with gray.

LE STERILIZZAZIONI DELLA realtà
puntando il dito alla tua faccia
e scivolando rivoltosi verso
quell'altro avvenire
spolvera docilmente a notte
tardissima,
parole poverissime nel loro abito dimesso.

La primavera docile segnalava
la burrasca fitta o fittizia
le tue querele o vincite fittizie,
follemente si innamora di te
voglia di rifare tutto il discorso,
semplificando il destino a poche
parole piatte.

Non si staccò mai da te nell'ombra
sofisticata della tua età marcia.

STERILIZATIONS OF REALITY
pointing a finger in your face
and sliding turned towards
that other future
dusts docilely so late
at night,
poorest words in their humble garb.

The docile spring signaled
the thick or fictitious storm
your complaints or fictitious winnings,
madly falls in love with you
wishing to do it all over again,
simplifying destiny to a few
flat words.

Never left you in the sophisticated
shadows of your rotten age.

SORTONO GLI ANGIOLI
bianchi e blu
e io seggo al balcone
bianco e nero

Crisi di bovarismo
crisi di impoverimento!
crisi di fiori
crisi di lavoratori

Il dialogo si fa a quattro
come una diagonale
descrivo autobus
mi rimetto in moto
altre preghiere
perché gli alberi sono blu?

(Le cose stesse
seminano il mio cuore di luce)

THE ANGELS ARE leaving
white and blue
and I sit on the balcony
black and white

Crisis of Bovarism
crisis of impoverishment!
crisis of flowers
crisis of workers

Four-way dialogue
like a diagonal
I describe buses
I get back on track
other prayers
why are the trees blue?

(Things themselves
sow my heart with light)

DEI TRADITORI
sapessi congiungere gli scopi
un fiore dondolante sull'altura
bianchissimi paesaggi senza cura
nessuna risposta dai villeggianti
e un alfiere da combattere *sine
die*, con quell'altura...
Hanno intonato un altro canto...
eri lontano
una cresta bianca
un allontanamento
una ringhiera solida
un allentamento
per poi buttarsi di nuovo nel
silenzio abbeverato di cortesia.

OF TRAITORS
if I knew how to unite their goals
a swaying flower on the heights
whitest heedless landscapes
no response from the sojourners
and a knight to fight *sine
die*, with those heights...
They intoned another song...
you were distant
a white crest
a distancing
a stout railing
a releasing
to then jump back into the
silence watered with courtesy.

COME SE SAPESSI cosa vuol dire l'opposto
cose lontanissime nella piccola patria
outside la foresta, e dai tropicali mucchi
nel *beige* del tricolore
morgana dalle ali incorrotte
nella povertà divenuta oramai orrido canile
vittima che eterna il suo male
come se da questo rinascesse verità stonando
con l'aria putrida di queste facce perse
nell'ora non romantica della tardissima mattina
e se ora tu dicessi
quel che non convenientemente si dice
in poesia?

As if I knew what the opposite meant
things so distant in the small homeland
outside the forest, and from the tropical heaps
in the *beige* of the tricolor
fairy of the uncorrupted wings
in a poverty by now like a horrid kennel
victim perpetuating its evil
as if from this the truth revived out of tune
with the putrid air of these lost faces
in the unromantic hour of late morning
and what if you'd now say
what is not conveniently said
in poetry?

SENZA UN GOCCIO di bellezza
la mia bellezza; senza nuore
senza compagnia la mia
stravagante passiva artiglieria:

contiamo passatempi e li
scontiamo – presi da un delirio
comune.

Quanta salsa e quanto coraggio!
Pupazzi grandiosi hanno grandioso

l'avvenire.

WITHOUT A DROP of beauty
my beauty; without daughters-in-law
without company my
extravagant passive artillery:

we count pastimes and
discount them—caught up in a common
delirium.

So much sauce and so much courage!
Grand puppets have grand

futures.

SE HAI DA nutrire il tuo sangue
mettendo tra le dita le mie dita:

Se hai da scordare il tuo sangue
mentendo come si fa in tempo

per la prosecuzione della battaglia:

Se hai da scalfire il tuo tempo
se hai da inorridire nel tuo

tempio...

IF YOU MUST feed your blood
sliding my fingers between your fingers:

If you must forget your blood
lying as you'll do in time

for the continuation of the battle:

If you must tarnish your time
if you must be horrified in your

shrine…

MORISTI ANCHE TU; o volesti morire, io
ne seppi notizia prima di morirne, semmai
fosti tu a darmela.

Ho la noia per traguardo, e la colpa
per retroguardia.

Tangente diviso, sono grottesca stasera
e gli orologi con i loro molti oggetti
non si stancano di guardare...

YOU TOO DIED; or wanted to die, I
heard about it before dying of it, if anything
you were the one letting me know.

Boredom is my target, and guilt
my rear guard.

Divided tangent, I'm grotesque tonight
and clocks with their many objects
they never tire of looking...

I VOSTRI SQUISITI confetti consolano,
madama, e coi vostri riccioli grigi apparecchiate
regalmente la tavola delle lacrime finte.

Il mio mestiere! – scoprirlo poi un vaniloquio
di sordità avvelenate, e rivalità soltanto
il tuo abbarbicare alla penna. Non basta!

sporgersi dal finestrino dell'amicizia:
dirsi ben altro – fu tutta la mia amicizia.

Your exquisite confections console,
madame, and with your gray curls you regally
set the table of feigned tears.

My trade!—discovering it later a vanity
of poisoned deafness, and sole rivalry
your clinging to the pen. It's not enough!

leaning out of the friendship window:
saying so much more—such was my friendship.

Ho lasciato in giro la gente: le pantofole
ora cerco te o un altro, e sei scomparso.
Era per vanità che siedevi su quel trono
che so che non ti porta?

Hai sete e vesti addosso: ti martori
di domande, fai il finto ossequioso, magari
la ricetta è un'altra –

Ho finito di scrivere, e continuo!

I LEFT PEOPLE lying about: my slippers
now I look for you or another, and you're gone.
Was it for vanity you sat on that throne
I know can't hold you?

You're parched and garbed: you martyr
yourself with questions, pretend to be obsequious
maybe there's another cure—

I'm done writing, and I resume!

IL PERCHÉ DELLE bufere: si sono stese
stamani grigie come se in odio a questo
respirare forse, anzi certamente troppo
speranzoso. Si sono stese nuvole e soffi
di venti d'altro ponente o emisfero e
noi correvamo tutti dietro alla pioggia
che però si rifiuta.

Siamo tutti inquilini ora, oggi – di questa
passione ad un odio per noi stessi, tanto

sicuri che tanto domani sarà peggio, e
lo stesso. O se fosse meglio? – allora
davvero avremmo da ridire e a contare
i nostri atti inforchettati, illusi, smorti
di ragionamenti a catena, tanto per seminare
più odio, e distruggere anche la speranza,
perfino le piccole speranze.

Cercavamo ieri sera una biforcazione
non una strada di campagna netta o cittadina
ma un semplice passaggio: vi ritrovammo
la morte! come sempre, la morte! Quasi

banale lo scoprirla intatta dopo tanti
anni di massonerie... E fingevamo d'averla
superata, ridimensionata, oppure valutata
appieno: fa sempre paura, invece, e tutto
fa paura se è nullo. Volemmo tutto nullo
e tutto fu nullo per il nulla finale
che volemmo sotto sotto. E pastorale
ora decantarsi, o decantare morte? Pastorale
salvare quelle poche rime molto standardizzate

THE REASON FOR the storms: they've spread
this morning gray as if hating perhaps
this breathing, actually too
hopeful by far. Clouds have spread and puffs
of wind of another west or hemisphere and
we all ran after the rain
that however refuses.

We're all tenants now, today—of this
passion for a hatred of ourselves, so

certain that tomorrow will be worse, and
the same. Or what if it were better?—then
we'd really have to object and count
our forked feats, fooled, dull
from chain reasoning, just to sow
more hatred, and destroy hope too,
even faint hopes.

We were looking for a crossing last night
not a clear country road nor a city street
but a simple passage: we found
death! as always, death! Almost

banal to discover it intact after so many
years of freemasonry... And we pretended to have
overcome it, scaled back, or completely
evaluated it: but it's always scary, and everything
is scary if it's null. We wanted it all null
and all was null for the final null
that deep down we wanted. And pastoral
decanting now, or decanting death? Pastoral
saving of those few so standardized rhymes

che soffocammo per riderne meglio, poi
imbarazzati di queste nostre curiose
scelte giovanili – sempre le stesse poi
a cicli conclusi e infiniti.

we choked back to laugh harder at them, then
embarrassed by our curious
youthful choices—always the same then
with full and infinite cycles.

IN QUESTO DESERTO dell'anima che mi anima
in questo fanciullesco scevrarsi da te
da me e da tutti gli altri (ti rifiutano)
nacqui al Fatebenefratelli, come se sulla
punta di un ago.

Avvelenandolo poi non seppi resistervi
(avevate già pianificata la pace) e allora
conobbi (analizzandoli con il cuore
in mano) anch'io i vostri metodi nel

tentativo di sorvolarvi. Psicologia spicciola
psicologa per una giornata: fraintesa
e magnificata al punto d'essere lillipuziana
afformicata come voi.

Ho preso servizio stasera e mi danno
uno stipendio.

In this desert of the spirit that inspires me
in this youthful severing from you
from me and everyone else (they refuse you)
I was born at the Fatebenefratelli, as if on the
tip of a needle.

Poisoning it then I couldn't resist it
(you'd alrcady planned peace) and so
I too experienced (analyzing them heart
in hand) your methods in an

attempt to overlook you. Petty psychology
psychologist for a day: misunderstood
and magnified to the point of being Lilliputian
insected like you.

I started tonight and they put me
on salary.

TENTO UN MERCATO – poi ne tento un altro
sorvolo sulle difficoltà e poi vi rimango
impantanata: è come dire, sì, se mi volete
sarò come voi: la stessa pasta ai vostri
affetti da ventriloqui!

Poeticamente si scansa, tenta il massimo
ancóra più ambigua: non ha fine la ricerca
di chi sta bene.

Dieci scellini all'anno assicurano la
sopravvivenza, se bene accalappiata,
destreggiata servirvi come se lavorassi.

Soldi situati nel minimo organizzabile
per commentare poi la situazione da voi
spalancata, su questi abissi che sono
l'urlare in punto di morte per non morire
di inedia o di scoraggiamento: nessuno

vuole i tuoi sporchi versi: mentre fai
il verso a Fidel, o a qualche altra scelta
d'eroizzare la tua esistenza appena tracciata.
Tenti altri eroi, altri sacrifici finché
t'accorgi che non ti vogliono, e la rivoluzione
poi non esiste, è tutta da farsi, non

certo da noi. Allora anzi decidi di separarti
fra due assurdi è preesistente il primo
fra due stranezze scegliere la meno bella

e spiegarti così, come se te lo chiedessero
(e infatti oggi tutto è mercato). Ma

I TRY OUT a market—then I try another one
I overlook the difficulties and then I'm
stuck: it's like saying, sure, if you want me
I'll be like you: the same cloth for your
ventriloquist affections!

Poetically she sidesteps, tries her best
even more ambiguous: the search is endless
for whoever is fine.

Ten shillings a year ensure
survival, if well ensnared,
skillfully serving you as if I were working.

Money situated in the minimum wave
to comment on the situation you
flung open, on these abysses
howling on the verge of death so as not to die
of starvation or discouragement: nobody

wants your filthy verses: while you
parrot Fidel, or some other choice
to heroize your newly formed existence.
You try out other heroes, other sacrifices until
you realize they don't want you, and revolution
doesn't exist, it's yet to be waged, certainly

not by us. So then you decide to divide yourself
between two absurdities the former is preexistent
between two oddities choosing the least beautiful

and explaining yourself this way, as if they asked you
(and in fact today everything is a market). But what

se tutto è stato e sarà sempre mercato?
Se volendo il mercato ti ritrovi rivoluzionario
e volendoti rivoluzionario-capo ti ritrovi

mercato? Nulla volle la volontà ma si
spostò da un canale all'altro, misteriosamente
la Sua volontà si fece, a cambiar l'altro
(il mondo intero fa come te, se può) perché
certamente ciò che aveva deciso era ciò
(come se per caso). Esitante ti riscrivi
o riiscrivi all'aristocrazia-élite dei
cervelli artistici: nessun conto in banca
ma quel minimo assicurato ti predestina
al forgiarsi rivoluzioni dei contenuti
e tentativi di rivoluzione *nei* contenuti.

if everything has been and always will be a market?
If wanting the market you find yourself a revolutionary
and wanting to be a revolutionary leader you find yourself

a market? The will wanted nothing but
shifted mysteriously from one channel to the next
His will be done, to change the other
(the whole world acts like you, or tries) because
certainly what had been decided was this
(as if by chance). Hesitantly you rewrite yourself
or reprise the aristocracy-elite of the
artistic brains: no bank account
but that guaranteed minimum destines you
to forge revolutionary content
and revolutionary attempts *in* content.

IL DIALOGO È oramai tra due o tre persone
che si tengono a distanza e sognano di
non conoscersi più, scrivendosi domande
e risposte per scolpire dentro questa
naturale biografica negatività.

A chi parlo? A un esperto scelto dalla
mia immaginazione, o è un passatempo
per i giornali?

Finché tutto sarà mondo e microscopico
nel grande non andare se ti fa male, coi
piccioncini che giuocano a fare da lustrascarpe
inginocchiandosi severi alle puttane
seminando infatti quesiti e risposte

e intascando i *veri* conti in banca!

(Puoi almeno dire di essere in mezzo
al cammin di nostra vita!)

By now the dialogue is between two or three people
who keep their distance and dream of
no longer knowing one another, writing questions
and answers to one another to sculpt into this
natural biographical negativity.

Who am I talking to? To an expert chosen by
my imagination, or is it a pastime
for the press?

Until all will be world and microscopic
in the big don't go if it hurts you, with
lovebirds playing shoeshine
kneeling harshly before the whores
in fact sowing questions and answers

and pocketing the *real* bank accounts!

(At least you can say you're midway
through the journey of our life!)

IL TUO BIONDO cenere
mi riduce in ceneri

compari, scompari, poi
non sai nemmeno se

hai qualche interesse
a incoraggiarmi, nemmeno
fai cenno.

E io che ti ricordo
in ogni dettaglio, viventissimo
con significati grandi
o piccoli assieme, di

cui tu non sai niente!

YOUR ASH-BLONDE
reduces me to ashes

you appear, disappear, then
you don't even know if

you've any desire
to encourage me, nor give
some sign.

And I remember you
in such detail, so vividly
with big meanings
or small together, of

which you know nothing!

È AMORE SEMPLICE, questo
disperarsi: è proprio

quello che chiamano
amore? – o è necessità
di costruire ingenuamente
nell'altro quello che

ti manca? Valori ovvii
o costruiti dalla mia

affamata mente?

It's simple love, this
despair: is it really

what they call
love?—or is it necessity
of building naively
in the other what

you're missing? Obvious values
or built by my

hungrymind?

Se sinistramente, ti vidi
apparire, come un sole nero
la tua biondezza, e il sole
recuperava tutto – o quasi

il tutto che in te trovai...

Un tutto che è mascherata
un tutto che è bisogno: semmai

era anche disperante, ritrovarsi
tali e quali all'adolescente

che mai crebbe: un sentimento
di devozione, è tutto ciò

che m'addombra... nell'ammiccare
per una fiotta di baci che

mai desti, né darai ora che
so quanto luminosa era per
me la tua figura sfocatamente
giustiziera, e lo spirito che
tramortendo la vita che
come sempre, scartando le
molte speranze s'annunciava
già pronta a rinunciare, magari
morendo nello sforzo di non
distinguere tra te e il male...

Però questa ennesima volta
veramente hai saputo riconoscerla
come tale. Butti via le speranze

IF SINISTERLY, I saw you
appearing, like a black sun
your blondness, and the sun
recovered everything—or almost

all that I found in you...

An all that's masquerade
an all that's need: if anything

it was also despairing, to find oneself
just like the adolescent

who never grew up: a feeling
of devotion, that's all

that shades me... winking
for a shoal of kisses

you never gave, nor will you ever give
now that I know how bright it was for
me your blurry executioner
figure, and the spirit
deadening life that
as always, discarding the
many hopes announced itself
already ready to give up, maybe
dying in the attempt of not
distinguishing between you and evil...

But this umpteenth time
you really knew how to recognize it
as such. You throw away your hopes

non sono altro che una fiotta
di baci ingenui e semplici
mentre nel male il vivere
si fa complesso, e ardendo
d'un nulla che è tutto il
mio pieno, la mia bislacca
vita in un mercato che ha
anch'esso il suo destinato
amore di copulazione, si farebbe

come tale la vuoi, disdegnando
d'insegnarmela!

they're nothing but a shoal
of naive and simple kisses
while in the evil living
becomes complex, and burning
with a nothing that's all
my plenty, my quirky
life in a market that too
has its inevitable
love of copulation, would be

just as you want it, disdaining
to teach it to me!

I GIOVANI, LE loro rose

simili a te: i giovani
le loro rose, simili

a me: i giovani, i loro
torti, simili ai nostri

THE YOUNG, THEIR roses

akin to you: the young
their roses, akin

to me: the young, their
faults, akin to ours

COLLARE DI SOSTEGNO e perdifiato, filato
il cordoglio grande la gioia, di vederti
stramazzare al suolo.
 Che colore eccentrico: che primavera!
Sono i tram e gli autobus, che non smettono
di piangere. Rumore o rotolìo inutile

il sangue degli orgasmi è ormai lontano
i sonni sono devoluti alla pazienza, e
la mia tristezza non ha pazienza... Oh

fingo d'essere me stessa e sono fra gli
altri, ben più paziente che la pazienza
di questo mio giorno tutt'intero devoluto

all'arte della pazienza. Ho trent'anni!
e collimo i versi rannicchiandomi tuttora

tra le seggiole d'un buon mercato a tutti
gli usi –

Support collar and dead run, spun
the grief great the joy, to see you
collapse to the ground.

What an eccentric color: what a spring!
Trams and buses, they don't stop
crying. Useless rumbling or rolling

the blood of orgasms is far away by now
dreams have devolved to patience, and
my sadness is out of patience... Oh

I pretend to be myself and I'm among the
others, far more patient than patience
with this whole day all devolved

to the art of patience. I'm thirty!
and I align the verses still curling up

between the chairs of a cheap all-purpose
market—

COME LE PIETRE sono con voi! – come le
pietre! – sono tutte lì, i pezzetti mancanti
e io sono qua ad attendere con loro, i

vostri bisogni: faticare per poi ricordare
di non essere più sorella ai vostri mostri

se non in un infinito pietriscolo d'alvare
se non in una sabbia mobile e fine come

questa scienza che un dì mi progredì.
Come le pietre ritengo utile e mio dovere

stabilire se in questo aldilà della realtà
v'è altro aldilà: che stinge e corrode
questo fraseggiare ignobile, questo credersi

cantanti di prose o prosodie: senza
poi mentire a sé o agli altri, partecipo

a tutti i vostri programmi...
Diurni, i rinfreschi serali non hanno
botte per i piatti o i pianti delle miracolate

trinità: marito moglie e pietre al collo
sono i diamanti dell'esistenza: io sono
quello che mai sapeste e poteste sapere

io sono come voi quel che non sapeste
mai mai mai svaligiai la banca, un permesso
chiesi per ricostruirla, come voi seppi

poi ritirarmi in tempo! (Nel buio della

How like the stones I am with you!—how like the
stones!—they're all there, the missing pieces
and I'm here awaiting with them, your

needs: trying hard to remember
not to be a sister to your monsters anymore

if not in an infinite graveled hive
if not in a mobile sand fine as

this science I made headway with one day.
Like the stones I deem useful and my duty

to determine if in this hereafter of reality
there's another hereafter: fading and corroding
this ignoble phrasing, this believing ourselves

singers of prose or prosody: without
lying to ourselves or others, I take part

in all your plans...
Daytime, evening refreshments don't have
a cask for plates or plaints of the miraculously healed

trinities: wife husband and millstones round the neck
are the diamonds of existence: I'm
the one you never knew nor could have known

I'm like you what you didn't know
never ever ever did I rob the bank, I asked
for a permit to rebuild it, like you I knew

how to withdraw in time! (In the dark of the

profonda cella si rimò d'incanto, d'accordo
con mura spente o limacciose, se uno

scritto sapeva essere lenza ad un futuro?
Futuro senza nome o speranza è gioia
di una morte senza speranze, è gioia
smettere di fingere di amare o di singhiozzare
è buia la scala fino all'androne, ed è
neghittosa la stanza poi raggiunta, poi
se mai vi poneste caso semmai era poi

con questa cruda eredità che vi ereditai.)

deep cell we rhymed wonderfully, in harmony
with extinguished or slimy walls, if

writing knew how to hook the future?
Future without a name or hope is joy
for a death without hope, it's joy
to stop pretending to love or to sob
the stairway is dark up to the lobby, and it's
neglectful the room later reached,
and if you ever paid heed if anything

I inherited you with this raw inheritance.)

SUPPORSI INTERAMENTE DISTRUTTI, fare
di tutto per abbreviare il percorso che
non corrisponde alle aspettative. Questo

era nelle intenzioni primariamente e
poi salutammo la folla.

Ma nella folla covavano serpentini stanamenti
ciò che avrebbe dovuto essere quello

che più ti preme: fu invece villania
giuoco e ristretta vendetta di pochi
vendicando l'innocente, in nome di una

spenta civiltà. Vendetta e calcoli sapevano
giurare, in nome d'un popolo misinterpretato
e assente: sporgere la mano significava

distruggersi, per lo spazio usufruito
da chi comanda, vuole comandare scartando

ogni futura verità.

PRESUMING TO BE entirely destroyed, do
everything to shorten the path that
fails to meet expectations. This

was the main intention and
then we greeted the crowd.

But in the crowd lurked sneaky flushings out
what should have been what

matters most to you: it was rather rudeness
a game and restricted revenge of a few
avenging the innocent, in the name of a

spent civilization. Calculated revenge they knew
how to swear, in the name of a misinterpreted
and absent people: sticking out one's hand meant

destroying oneself, for the space taken
by those in charge wishing to command discarding

every future truth.

Non è vero che correndo si distingue
non correggeva la natura la sua iperbole
la realtà vivendosi da sola
non ebbe pace finché non si ritrovò sbendata
grande marcia contro il trionfatore, padre
di tutti i nostri alberghi, albergatori
segretamente innamorati tutti della miseria
di questi nostri cento giorni distratti
mani direttamente coinvolte nello sporchissimo
modo di costruirci che abbiamo.

Poesia difficile queste semplicissime
parole un difficilissimo ricatto
la mente tardiva non esplora altro
semmai foste semplicemente voi stessi
a servire il popolo che vi stana e giudica.

IT'S NOT TRUE that by running it stands out
nature didn't correct its hyperbole
reality living by itself
knew no peace until it found itself unblindfolded
great march against the victor, father
of all our hotels, hoteliers
all secretly in love with the misery
of these our hundred distracted days
hands directly involved in the dirty
way to devise ourselves that we have.

Difficult poem these very simple
words a most difficult blackmail
the belated mind explores nothing else
if anything you were simply the ones
serving the people who flush you out and judge you.

per Gianfranco

Non ho voglia di morire oggi, non ho nemmeno
speranza di morire oggi: sono in piena
attività cerebrale; sono come gli altri –

candida, della tua morte fiorita d'oltretombe
della tua morte offerta a premio, del

tuo intimidito sorriso giovanile, della
tua sfacciataggine sicura e spretata. Sono

sicura tu cambierai registro, sono sicurissima
che non mi amerai neppure là, dove vai
e dove andrò io, vivente. Sei mai sicuro

tu di questa stessa cosa, faccenda, delirante
sicurezza d'invecchiare?

(«Non sono sicura d'esserti vicino, mai
ho sicurezza intera di te, che spiando
mi ragguagli o raggiungi... Competizione!
la vita senza guinzagli, garbugli, gola
o freschezza impervia». Deliravo, e mi
misi ad armeggiare per correggere questo

vizio... di saperti armato di sapienza
di saperti lontano un quarto di miglia

come se tutta la sapienza al mondo potesse
sbranar cani come io già sto facendo, come

for Gianfranco

I don't want to die today, I've no
hope of dying today: I'm in full
throttle; I'm like the others—

candid, of your flowered death of afterlives
of your death offered as a prize, of

your shy youthful smile, of your
defrocked and frank cheekiness. I'm

certain you'll switch gears, I'm quite certain
that you won't love me even there, where you go
and where I'll go, living. Are you certain

of this same thing, matter, delusional
certainty of aging?

("I'm uncertain of being close to you, never
do I feel wholly certain of you, who spying
brief or reach me… Competition!
life unleashed, snarls, throat
or impervious freshness." I was delirious, and I
started tinkering to correct this

vice… of knowing you armed with wisdom
of knowing you a quarter of a mile away

as if all the wisdom in the world could
mangle dogs as I'm already doing, as

io già farò, riposandomi in questa baracca
riposandomi in ricerca di te che muori

quasi allegramente. – Perché, tanto sorriso
e tanta educazione? Nei sorrisi arabescati

del vino fluente e secco, superbo il
vino ma mista la miscela!

E sono morta oramai vicino al tuo scoccare
frecce intere per il mio parmigiano, nel
ridere di vita e morte interezza e spugne
non ho più nulla da dire, come te, che
spari o sparisci.)

I'll certainly do, resting in this hovel
resting in search of you who die

almost cheerfully.—Why such a big smile
and such courtesy? In the arabesque smiles

of the flowing and dry wine, superb the
wine but mixed the mixture!

And I'm dead by now near your striking
whole arrows for my parmesan, in
laughing at life and death wholeness and sponges
I've nothing more to say, like you, who
fire or flee.)

SOFFIAVA LA FAME ed era estrema, sintomo
o singulto (singolare) d'una estrema
passione, sincera – col suo stendere

abiti iconoclastici per terra e sul
marciapiede – d'un valore perduto e distantemente

quello che avresti voluto fare. Sincerità
(oh singulto dell'ultima passione), sincera
era, nel suo svegliarsi all'ora proibita

e nel cavare, da ogni spazzola o dentifricio
quello che poteva essere l'ora buona
il momento inafferrabile ora che è delicata

la faccenda; e contavi le ore, d'un tuo
possibile premio, e contavi l'avvenire
come se fosse monetine!

HUNGER HUFFED AND was extreme, symptom
or sobbing (singular) of an extreme
passion, sincere—with its trailing

iconoclastic gowns on the floor and on the
sidewalk—of a lost value and distantly

what you'd wanted to do. Sincerity
(oh sobbing of the last passion), she was
sincere, in her awakening at the forbidden hour

and in digging out, from every brush or toothpaste
what could be the right moment
the elusive hour now that it's a delicate

matter; and you counted the hours, of your
possible prize, and you counted the future
as if it were coins!

COLLE DI LIMONE: solitudine
impeccabile! pregno di luce

sono io stasera: non buia
la verde estate o estatica

la marcia violetta alla
vendetta...

LEMON HILL: IMPECCABLE
solitude! imbued with light

I am tonight: not dark
the green estate or ecstatic

the violet march towards
vendetta...

Il Cristo (Pasqua 1971)

Perché morendo ci fai venir a festa? Semmai
era l'*altro* lato che andava premiato
e tu non rifiutasti quel cibo acerbo
vinaigre di festa e botte sulle spalle

pacchie e grandiose costruzioni per la
mente intorbidita: i cinque sensi hanno

dunque così poco conto o peso che tu

vaneggi su croce elegante e di legno?

Se di legno marcisci non lamentare quel
tuo dolore alle spalle: esse fanno sì
che tu operoso insoddisfatto però rimi
come se fosse prima: e inoltre lezioni

dai del tuo operato costosissimo, nel
vaneggiare di cose insapori e digerite

così come la finalità di tutte le cose
così come il conto festoso e a rima quando

ti precipiti al balcone, dal balcone
per vederti camminare.

The Christ (Easter 1971)

Why do you make us rejoice by dying? If anything
it was the *other* side that had to be rewarded
and you didn't refuse that unripe food
festive *vinaigre* and shouldered cask

bounty and grandiose constructions for the
turbid mind: the five senses are

thus of so little account or weight that you

rave on an elegant wooden cross?

If of wood you rot don't complain about
that ache in your shoulders: they ensure
that hardworking dissatisfied nonetheless
you rhyme as before: and also you give

lessons of your most costly work, in
raving at tasteless and digested things

as well as the goal of all things
as well as the festive and rhyming count when

you rush the balcony, from the balcony
to see yourself walking.

PAROLE PACIFICHE
sono incastrate nel nulla
ho riminiscenze del tutto
e non so tutto

Parole nel nulla! – non
voglio esclamare: sono
atrofizzata, e non c'è

nulla da fare.

Peaceful Words
they're stuck in nothingness
I reminisce about the whole
and don't know all

Words in nothingness!—I don't
want to exclaim: I'm
atrophied, and

nothing to be done.

FACILE FARE
quello che si vuol fare

difficile essere
proprio quel che si vuol essere.

(Paradisi Perduti) –
ecco il mio assioma

son senza cella certa
e son senza paradiso.

Ma che passione al bello!
Ma che convenzione al buono!

(Sono io che guido
e sei tu che obbedisci.)

EASY TO DO
what you want to do

difficult to be
just what you want to be.

(Lost Paradises)—
here's my axiom

I lack a clear cell
and I'm without paradise.

But what a passion for beauty!
But what a convention for good!

(It's me guiding
and it's you obeying.)

HO NELLA STELLA nera del mio destino
un qualche cosa che non è questo
versificare per buone donne o fanti
o spente illuse stelle silenziose
o rauche vanità d'essere additata
tra i primi.

In capo al masto, che scotendosi
s'adattava bene a tutti i venti
e silenziosamente sempre rimontava
tu ti penti.

Ma ora hai scelto magnificamente
la tua sorte: sortendo tra i sorteggi
un bacio immaginario, tutto un
trainare di distinzioni, sfumate
e elefantiche.

Direttamente nel vuoto del fango
mai alzare voce, infatti: quando
sostando vicino alla tua passione
la bruciasti.

IN THE BLACK star of my destiny
I've got something that's not this
versifying for beauty queens or jacks
or silent spent illusory stars
or hoarse vanity of being singled out
among the first.

At the top of the mast, which by shaking
suited all winds well
and always silently remounted
you repent.

But now you've brilliantly chosen
your fate: by drawing among the draws
an imaginary kiss, a whole
dragging of distinctions, shaded
and elephantic.

Straight in the mud void
never raise your voice, in fact: upon
drawing close to your passion
you burned it.

CONTINENZA EUROPEA, SEMMAI venne
con un carico di bestiame
come la terapia della scienza
che fu questo nostro pensare ogni
dì, la libertà di pensare.

Si travagliavano in vano corto
e spento quel che mai fu scritto
su di creta neutra
egiziana inaspettata
o semplicemente ambizione di propria
voce?

Quattro stanze indivisibili
quattro angoli nascostissimi
polvere o grigiore e smemoratezza
v'hanno composto questa ballata
(angoli delle mie quattro stanze)
non disturba il vostro io trafelato

non volge in canto forte.

European continence, if anything it came
with a load of cattle
like the science therapy
that was our thinking every
day, the freedom of thinking.

They labored in vain short
and spent what had ever been written
on neutral unexpected
Egyptian clay
or simply ambition of their own
voice?

Four indivisible stanzas
four innermost corners
dust or grayness and forgetfulness
have composed this ballad for you
(corners of my four stanzas)
doesn't disturb your out-of-breath self

doesn't turn into loud song.

NON RESISTI A quest'inverno
modestamente
quel fango innocente
e con le scarpe in mano
e nudo attraversi
quella piazza,
viaggiare per piazze.

YOU CAN'T WITHSTAND this winter
modestly
that innocent mud
and with shoes in hand
and naked you cross
that square,
traveling across squares.

NEL NORDICO
palmeto di chiese sconsacrate,
forzate risate
la città in palmo,
vita da carbonizzare

IN THE NORDIC
palm grove of deconsecrated churches,
forced laughter
the city in the palm,
charred life

SAPERSI MOLTO VICINI alle
retrovie dei ragazzi «in
panne», e pur sapendo, reagendo

presentarsi nuda al televisore
consumando «arte e storie»

d'una altra età giovanile
quella che è vostra e mostruosamente

si evolve ad essere mia.

FEELING VERY CLOSE to
the "stranded" youth behind
the lines, and yet reacting

showing up naked on TV
consuming "art and stories"

of another young age
the one that's yours and monstrously

evolves to be mine.

Neve 1973

Neve, a bricconi sulla pianta della testa
rivoluzione pesante delle maniere, manierismo
anche quello se tu non puoi più andare

avanti col soliloquio (arancione naturalmente)
così come avevi condotto a sperare. Non

puoi più mentire a te stessa! – s'è scippata
la burrasca, e t'hanno chiuso dentro per
farti meglio ragionare.

Io non sono quello che apparo – e nel bestiame
d'una bestiale giornata a freddo chiamo
voi a recitare.

Snow 1973

Snow, crooked on the sole of the head
weighty revolution of manners, mannerism
even that one if you can't move forward

any longer with the soliloquy (orange of course)
just as you had led to hope. You

can't lie to yourself any longer!—she snatched up
the blizzard, and they locked you in
to help you think better.

I'm not what I appear—and among the beasts
of a beastly cold day I call
upon you to recite.

E NELL'ACQUEDOTTO
si rintanano le rane, hanno spulciato
anche loro le acque
in attesa
d'una divorazione semplice
sanno che tu sgarri
come prima, come
se fosse
nel tuo vivere naturalissimo
scambiare rane per acqua.

Veloci foglie
sentitemi arrancare
non ho la vostra pazienza –
rimugino sino in fondo
le salde attese.

AND IN THE aqueduct
frogs hole up, they've combed
their waters as well
waiting
for a simple devouring
they know you're messing up
as before, as
if it were
most natural in your living
exchanging frogs for water.

Quick leaves
hear me trudge
I lack your patience—
brooding to the end
the firm expectations.

CORRUZIONE NEL GIORNALE di ieri
centoventimila tiratori scelti.

Senza lezione
scemava nella tenerezza costrittiva
l'inconscia palla del nemico divertito.

Sovente nell'arte illustrata
consiglio donò
scempio tutt'intero –

CORRUPTION IN YESTERDAY'S paper
one hundred twenty thousand snipers.

Without a lesson
waned in constrictive tenderness
the unconscious bullet of the amused enemy.

Often in illustrated art
advice was given
havoc run amuck—

Afterword

A trilingual writer who described herself as "a poet of exploration," Amelia Rosselli has only recently been recognized as one of the major European poets of the twentieth century. Born in Paris in 1930, she was the daughter of the martyred antifascist philosopher Carlo Rosselli and the British political activist Marion Cave. After her father's death in 1937, Amelia was raised in exile, in France, Switzerland, England, and the United States, before finally settling in Italy after the war, first in Florence and then in Rome. Except for a year she spent in London in the mid-seventies, Rosselli never left Rome. It was there that, after years of struggling with mental illness, which led to an increased sense of personal and literary isolation, she took her own life in 1996.

The tragedy of her father's assassination at the hands of the Fascists and the loss of her mother when she was only nineteen were central to Rosselli, defining her in many ways, from her "trilingual language" and cosmopolitan upbringing—though she thought of herself more as a refugee—to her political engagement and deep social consciousness (like many other Italian intellectuals of the postwar years, she was a member of the PCI, the Italian Communist Party). In a rare autobiographical passage from her first collection, *War Variations*, Rosselli describes her life thus:

> Born in Paris labored in the epos of our flawed
> generation. Lay in America among the rich fields of landlords
> and of the stately State. Live in Italy, barbaric country.
> Fled from England, country of sophisticates. Hopeful
> in the West where for now nothing grows.
>
> (trans. Re and Vangelisti)

Rosselli usually wrote effortlessly and with minimal revision. But it took her seven years to complete the process of selecting poems for her third major collection, Document. The chronological span of Document's poems runs from August 26, 1966, to May 18, 1973. The bulk of the book was written between 1966 and 1969. It was a monstrous undertaking, with more than 600 poems to choose from, "an ocean of material," as she put it to her brother John, with some of the discarded pieces ending up in a shorter follow-up collection, Notes Scattered and Lost. The final work, published by Garzanti in 1976, includes 175 poems ("a packed and luxuriant book," reads the jacket cover), chronologically ordered, as is customary for Rosselli. In the typescripts of her works, Rosselli usually added to her poems the date of their composition and an order number. From this, she claimed, "the development of soul and mind emerges, and the unconscious, in order to surface, must not do so abruptly; it does so slowly."[1]

In one of the few self-commentaries about her work, published in 1968 by the literary review La fiera letteraria, Rosselli described the book as "static, synthetic, perhaps icy and explosive at the same time: in short, a book of 'reached maturity.'"[2] As a matter of fact, after Document, there followed a long period of creative silence, only interrupted in 1979 by the long poem Impromptu. In a 1978 interview, after the publication of Document, Rosselli said that writing had now abandoned her, and so she had nothing left.[3] And even if this was only partially true, from then on she dedicated herself primarily to organizing, rearranging, and publishing her early writings. Document can therefore be considered a point of arrival in her poetry. This was also the only time, Rosselli said, that she structured a book before writing it. This makes perfect sense if we take at face value what she declared in more than one interview, that she took her inspiration from Petrarch's *Canzoniere* as an ideal model.

Rosselli had in fact long been fascinated by the classical sonnet, as opposed to free verse. Within the sonnet form, however, hers is an extremely inventive and daring poetic language, bursting with neologisms, puns, anagrams, portmanteaus, alliterations, dizzying associations, including those created from calques and loans from French and English, at times a truly linguistic Babel—as one scholar put it: "Associative competence is the real structuring principle of the text."[4] Precisely the constant drift from one tongue to the next, the often nonstandard use of syntax together with occasional spelling "mistakes," was what inspired Pier Paolo Pasolini's famous definition of Rosselli's language in terms of *lapsus*:

> One of the most sensational examples of Amelia Rosselli's linguistic connectives is the *lapsus* or Freudian slip. Sometimes false, sometimes true: but when false it is probably so in the sense that, having taken shape spontaneously, it is immediately accepted, adopted, and stuck by the author under the category of "self-made invention."[5]

Though Rosselli never agreed: "Mine are not lapsus, they are distortion games on words practiced with the overlapping of multiple languages, for it is not about unconscious improvisation."[6] It is not always easy to distinguish between deliberate and unintentional misspellings, which is probably why Italian editions have kept the occasional spelling errors, mostly double consonants, though sometimes incorrect verb conjugations.

In contrast to the boldness of her language is the regularity of her prosody, which Rosselli described in the theoretical essay "Metrical Spaces," written in response to Pier Paolo

Pasolini's request for clarification regarding her metrical system. In this innovative and difficult essay, Rosselli describes it as based on the word, any word, because any word is a sound, and, as such, words all hold the same value. Rosselli characterizes this system as composed of blocky stanzas suggesting a square, and thereby the Chinese ideogram. Most of Rosselli's poems use this form, and Rosselli was very particular about it to the point that on the occasion (and only on this occasion) of her second collection, *Hospital Series*, she was able to convince the publisher to use an IBM font, in which each letter takes up the same space, as most appropriate for reproducing her verses' cohesiveness. She envisioned the same graphic layout as well for *Document*, of which in a note addressed to a likely publisher she wrote:

> In *Document* I strictly adhered to my usual "closed" metrical system for about 60% of the poems. The other poems, apparently in a "free" style, are actually based on the same implied metrical system, but as if I had bitten off piles of images or sentences from the right margin of the poems, thus upsetting their geometric or "cubic" aspect.[7]

Let us now return to the idea of a *canzoniere*. Now, even if, in the Italian poetic tradition, a *canzoniere* is strictly speaking a collection of poems, it always reminds one of Petrarch's strong architectural structure: 366 poems (mostly sonnets) carefully ordered, telling the story of Petrarch's love for his muse Laura. In truth, more than a love story, Petrarch's *Canzoniere* is a sophisticated Augustinian reflection on the passage of time and on the dialectic between present, past, and future occasioned by the act of collecting fragments. By embracing the *Canzoniere* structure, Rosselli inscribes herself in this tradition, at the same time as she subverts it through the ordered chaos of her poetic language. At first glance, nothing seems to be further from *Document* than Petrarch's carefully arranged collection. However, Rosselli was aware of the interplay between autobiography (albeit highly idealized) and fiction in Petrarch's poetry, and she was fascinated by what it means to tell a story through a collection of poems— in Rosselli's story or stories, as in Petrarch's, autobiography is always knowingly lurking.

To summarize, we know that she organized her poems, and we are aware of the references they contain to each other, and of the importance of the chronology and the order they occupy within the collection. She even opens *Document* with a shortened sonnet whose syntax and lexicon are strongly reminiscent of Petrarch's first sonnet.[8] As in Petrarch, the syntax is "easy," as if to invite the audience (evoked at the end of both poems) to read it. The approach of the poet is one of looking back, an image of memory—even though, as is customary in Rosselli, this statement is two-faced, literally meaning, to turn one's back.

Poems collected in a *canzoniere* are often anthologized, but ideally, they should never be separated. Only by reading them one after the other can the reader follow the story or appreciate the motifs of groups of poems and find meaning in the way they are structured. Fragments themselves, so typical of Rosselli's writing and influenced by the avant-garde, are also somewhat inspired by Petrarch (whose *Canzoniere* was actually titled *Rerum Vulgarium Fragmenta*, meaning "Scattered rhymes in vernacular"). In fact, not only are certain of Rosselli's poems fragments per se, but much of her work utilizes collage of different fragments. Speaking of *Document*, Rosselli said:

> It was hard work; those who do not write poetry cannot imagine to what lengths poets go in order to compose,

even if they barely scrape by, and even if it's still the case that poetry is either inspired or worthless.⁹

This "hard work," one Rosselli was most fond of, resulted in the transformation of the literary model of her predecessor Petrarch into an innovative and ambitious venture reflecting the challenges of her own subjective experience—the pain, the intensity and turmoil of her existence—and our own violent chaotic times.

Roberta Antognini
Vassar College, 2024

Notes

All translations above are my own, except where noted. For full bibliographic information on works cited here, see the Bibliography.

1 From a 1995 interview (in Rosselli 2010, 178).
2 Rosselli 2004, 285.
3 Rosselli 2010, 25.
4 Agosti 1995, 134.
5 Pasolini 2005, 378.
6 Rosselli 2010, 165
7 Rosselli 2007, 38.
8 Petrarch's first sonnet as translated in "literal prose" by Robert M. Durling: "You who hear in scattered rhymes the sound of those sighs with / which I nourished my heart during my first youthful error, when / I was in part another man from what I am now: // for the varied style in which I weep and speak between vain / hopes and vain sorrow, where there is anyone who understands / love through experience, I hope to find pity, not only pardon. // But now I see well how for a long time I was the talk of the / crowd, for which often I am ashamed of myself within; // and of my raving shame is the fruit, and repentance, and the / clear knowledge that whatever pleases in the world is a brief / dream."
9 Rosselli 2010, 175.

Notes to the Poems

Over the last twenty years, Amelia Rosselli's works have enjoyed a steady stream of translations into English, a quite remarkable occurrence for a poet who is never "catchy," who engages her readers (and her translators) in hand-to-hand combat without a moment's respite. Many translators are in fact academics, which has made the scholarship around Rosselli both in the US and UK particularly vibrant. This is very good news for a poet whose mother was English, who lived in New York State for a few years, was fluent in English, and was herself a translator of poetry.

The translation of Rosselli continues to this day. In 2023, New York Review of Books published *Sleep*, Rosselli's collection of poems in English, for the first time outside of Italy. Now, with the publication of *Document*, only one of Rosselli's works remains unavailable in English, *Primi Scritti* (*First Writings*), though excerpts have been translated by Deborah Woodard and Giuseppe Leporace in *The Dragonfly*, Jennifer Scappettone in *Locomotrix*, and Roberta Antognini, Deborah Woodard, and Dario De Pasquale, in *Obtuse Diary*.

Each of *Document*'s poems deserves a note. But a commentary on such a large number of poems of this complexity would require another volume. We have included notes where we thought readers could benefit most from some contextual explanation, providing a few more tools with which to penetrate this complex work. (All translations from Italian in the notes that follow are our own, unless otherwise stated.)

<u>On the source text:</u>
Documento was first published in 1976 by Garzanti (Milan, Italy). For this bilingual volume, we follow the text as it appears in Amelia Rosselli's *L'opera poetica* (Milan: Mondadori, 2012).

<u>On Rosselli's punctuation:</u>
While some of Rosselli's poems lack punctuation entirely, others demonstrate her experimentation. In certain cases, her use of punctuation may seem arbitrary, leaving the reader somewhat disoriented

and questioning why she places a comma where it seems unnecessary or omits one where grammar would typically require it. It is important to keep in mind that Rosselli was not only a poet but also a musician and musicologist. Some of her commas are intentionally placed to create pauses, reflecting her sensitivity to rhythm and sound. In general, Italian and English punctuation rules are similar. Therefore, to offer English readers an experience as close as possible to that of the Italian readers, for the most part we have chosen not to alter her sometimes eclectic punctuation.

to Renato
Renato— Renato Gottuso (1911–1987), neorealist painter, a senator of the PCI, the Italian Communist Party, from 1976 to 1979. Gottuso and Rosselli had a difficult romantic relationship. He is most probably the addressee of the first few poems of the collection. This lover figure then turns into a father figure in the sonnet that begins "Oxygen in my curtains." When she was seven years old, Rosselli's father, the philosopher Carlo Rosselli, was assassinated in Paris, together with his brother Aldo, on the orders of the Italian Fascist government.

Stones turn taut in the woods…
Gross— Translated from *lordi*, a good example of the way Rosselli creates her "trilingual" lexicon, in this case using a Gallicism. In Italian *lordo* means "dirty," but it's most commonly used in the expression *peso lordo*, "gross weight"; whereas in French *lourde* means "heavy." Using *lordi* with the meaning of "heavy" allows Rosselli to end the poem with a pun on the verb *pesare*, "to weigh." We decided to translate *lordi* with "gross," which also has the meaning of "unpleasant." See the poem beginning "Verdigris-infused branch…," in which *lordo* has the same meaning as the French *lourde* and where both the verb *pesare/appensantire* (to weigh, to weigh down) and the semantic field of the forest (woods, branch, fir) appear again.

To Shubert
Shubert— Given the musical content of this poem, this is likely a misspelling of the musician Franz Schubert's name (see Afterword for

Rosselli's misspellings). Before devoting herself exclusively to poetry, Rosselli was a musicologist and a musician.

Concatenation of causes: you've seen the shadow
your brother— Rosselli was very close to her "brother in flesh" John, but here the "brother" is probably her "brother in spirit" or "friend brother," Rocco Scotellaro, the writer, poet, and politician with whom Rosselli had a great affectionate friendship and who died very young in 1954, provoking an unsurpassed pain for Rosselli, who remembered him for the rest of her life.

The hard life of the executed renovated
doléance— In Italian *doleanze* is a neologism, a calque from the French *doléance* (inspired by the famous *cahier de doléances*). In Italian, the correct translation for *doléance* would be *doglianza*.

A blue blue blue blue blue sea, even green
Figures of speech accumulate in the last stanza of this poem. It's not unusual for Rosselli to introduce variations that often become a conundrum for her translators. Take, for example, the expression **free wheelings**. Rosselli uses the plural: *ruote libere*. Typically, in the singular, this idiom matches up with the English expression "free-wheeling." We kept the plural and opted for two words instead of one in order to maintain the literal meaning, as Rosselli employs the expression to refer to the free wheels in a mechanism. The expression "freewheeling" also appears in the following poem, according to a system of correlation between poems common in Rosselli's collections, but particularly evident in *Document*.

I rhymed, toward a bank
rhymed— Another example of Rosselli's puns, and of the challenge of translating them. The first line of this poem reads in Italian: *Rimai, verso una proda*. It looks like an easy translation, except that with just a vowel change in the word *rimai*, we would have a completely different scenario: *remai*, "I rowed" (toward a bank).

Night, drawn labyrinth
the section is a deception— The meaning of this line is unclear, and the context doesn't help. We therefore opted for a literal translation. However, in Italian the word *sezione* could also mean the physical place, i.e., the building or room where meetings and political activities are held. Rosselli was politically active in the PCI, the Italian Communist Party, and we know that she frequented one of the Roman branches of the party, often taking care of even the humblest tasks.

Pines have sea nearby and warm sand
The last stanza describes a ride on a Piaggio Ciao scooter. A friend of Rosselli, Renzo Paris, notes in his book *Miss Rosselli*: "In 1968, Amelia divided her time between the party branch of the PCI and the demonstrations of the Student Movement. I often saw her on her bicycle following those noisy and violent demonstrations, in trousers and a cap with a visor. Sometimes she appeared with her Ciao, zigzagging to the sides of the rally like a dragonfly" (136). The comparison to a dragonfly is an allusion to Rosselli's long poem *The Dragonfly*.

And those kids have soft coats
pied— The adjective cangiante means "changing" but also "iridescent" (as in "iridescent eyes"). In translating the title of G.M. Hopkins's poem, "Pied Beauty," Eugenio Montale used the word *cangiante*, hence Rosselli's choice in Italian and our choice to translate it as "pied." Rosselli used this adjective a few other times in her works, but it's a hapax here in *Document*.

It's
for a loft stuffed with good books— For the last twenty years of her life Rosselli lived in a *mansarda* in Via del Corallo 25, a tiny, bare-bones loft near Piazza Navona, in Rome. Her books are now in the library of the University of Tuscia (Viterbo).

I've twenty days
my sententious little diary— One of Rosselli's metapoetic moments, where she defines the collection as a "diary," reminding the

reader of the "autobiographical" aspect of her *canzoniere*. This poem is part of a group of syntactically simpler poems, with a more accessible lexicon, and in which we find many of her recurring themes: politics (revolution, clenched fist, the enemy); the ever-present death (introduced by the cemetery); and the theme of her mental distress (the enemy tearing off her clothes, happiness/unhappiness).

A clenched / fist that ensures— One of the difficulties of translating Rosselli is the ambiguous use of the Italian personal pronouns, all the possibilities of which she exploits. Here in the second stanza, between the relative pronoun and the verb, there is the personal pronoun *le*: "un pugno / chiuso che le garantisce." *Le* could be a plural object pronoun referring to "words" (them)—in which case the reader should pause before the next line. Or it could be an indirect singular pronoun, *her*, referring to the poet herself, although the first-person possessive "my" in the following line seems to exclude that. In order to preserve the same ambiguity in English, often the best choice is not to translate the pronoun at all.

A thousand, small delicate objects...
This brief, pivotal poem, almost a sonnet but not quite, is strongly reminiscent of the first and last poems of Petrarch's *Canzoniere*. Both poets refer to personal experience: Petrarch says he is the "talk of the crowd"; Rosselli compares her life to a best seller. Both mention error and pardon (see note 8 in the Afterword for Petrarch's first sonnet). The poem also suggests the order and peace of Petrarch's last poem, the famous "Canzone to the Virgin." While Rosselli's is far from a religious perspective, she still refers to peace as "peace on earth," a decisively religious turn of phrase. The theme of error, of the fall, continues throughout the next poem, "Collapse" (one of the few with a title).

Once more I meddled
my raving— *Quel mio vaneggiare*, in Italian, is a quotation of the first sonnet of Petrarch's *Canzoniere*: "and of my raving, shame is the fruit" (*et del mio vaneggiar vergogna è il frutto*). In these central poems of the collection, Rosselli seems to refer with particular insistence to Petrarch.

Still before a destiny ever self-moving
In their final form, Rosselli did not number her poems, but we can't avoid counting them. This poem, a classical sonnet, is number 100 in this collection, a symbolic number, especially if we think of the calculated order of Petrarch's *Canzoniere*. It is a poem rich in self-referential allusions, to the struggle of earning a living (Rosselli fought all her life against poverty) and to her condition as a poet who writes of "indescribable things."

midday lull— The Italian *contr'ora* (spelled unusually—the word is a combination of *contro* and *ora*—usually *controra*) is an evocative term suggesting the cardinal sin of sloth: the early hours of the afternoon, especially in the summer, when it's too hot to do anything but rest. The demon in charge of tempting this sin is the so-called meridian demon, instiller of melancholy, who arouses visions, fantasies, restlessness, and a labored sleep full of hallucinations.

Had it been easier sharing you
Moon-boom— The translation of the expression *luna-boom* in the last verse is a perfect example of loss/gain in translation. In Italian *luna* has not only the literal meaning of moon, but also reminds one of *Luna Park* (after Coney Island, Luna Park is the general name for an amusement park in Italian), except that instead of *park*, Rosselli uses the word *boom*, a loan from English associated in Italian with the economic explosion of the fifties and sixties. In English we lose this association, but we gain in terms of sound with the lucky rhyme and consonance of *moon-boom*.

Fan-shaped alibis
laurels— Most of Petrarch's *Canzoniere* is dedicated to his muse, Laura. Laura's name is reminiscent of the laurel plant, sacred to the god Apollo and the symbol of glory. It suggests that writing about his love for Laura will give the poet glory. One of the ways Petrarch plays with Laura's name is by adding an apostrophe and transforming *Laura* in *l'aura*, a poetic term to indicate air. In this poem, Rosselli appropriates the term for herself, first in the proverbial expression "rest on your laurels," and then as a pun on the words *l'arena* (arena) and *la rena* (sand).

that morning after secretly
Many "leftovers" from *Document*, poems and fragments of poems, merged into the collection *Notes Scattered and Lost*, published a few years later, in 1983. However, Rosselli kept a few fragments in *Document*, possibly to add some variety to the collection, following the example of Petrarch, who in his *Canzoniere* included not only sonnets but also songs, *sestine*, ballads, and madrigals.

General Strike 1969
The so-called *autunno caldo* (hot autumn) of 1969, during which Italy was swept by a wave of protests and workers' union confrontations (fostered by the political climate of 1968) when millions of workers were waiting for their contracts to be renewed. On November 19, 1969, Italy came to a standstill. The strike was a huge success, with over 20 million public and private employees participating, and the country was paralyzed for 24 hours. In December, agreements were signed, especially for metalworkers who obtained a reduction in the working week to 40 hours, the right to assemble in the factory, significant wage increases, and the recognition of union representatives.

In this desert of the spirit that inspires me
Fatebenefratelli— Hospital in Rome, located on the western side of the Tiber Island, now called Fatebenefratelli Isola Tiberina. It's a popular hospital for births—although Rosselli was born in Paris. *Fatebenefratelli* is the term used for the monks belonging to the Hospital Order of St. John of God, an order devoted to the cause of the dying, the poor, the sick, and prostitutes. Its name means "do good, brothers," from the habit of the monks to invite benefactors to collaborate financially in the order's charitable works.

Your ash-blonde
For much of her life, Rosselli thought she was being spied on by the CIA, because of her father's and uncle's political past and her own membership in the PCI, the Italian Communist Party. Rosselli was frequently admitted to psychiatric clinics and was often subjected to electroshocks (mentioned for instance in the poem "Snow 1973":

"they locked you in / to help you think better). In this poem the "ash-blonde" man would be, in fact, a CIA agent (Paris 189–92).

If sinisterly, I saw you
Rosselli had a very particular voice, hoarse, deep, and with a slight French accent. In this YouTube video, you can hear her reading this poem in the original Italian: https://www.youtube.com/watch?v=tur8Ll4vVy4 (begins at 3′17″)

for Gianfranco
Gianfranco— Gianfranco Fiore Donati (1946–2022), director, screenwriter, and cinematographer. Rosselli met him in 1968 when Donati was a young militant in the PCI.

In the black star of my destiny
beauty queens or jacks— The expression *buone donne o fanti* is another example of Rosselli's ability to devise expressions with multiple meanings. In playing cards, *donne* and *fanti* are two of the face cards, queens and jacks. *Buone donne* means literally "good women," as well as "prostitutes." In English we transformed the prostitutes to beauty queens. We lost the literal meaning and changed the metaphor but were able to preserve the image of the cards.

feeling very close to
"stranded," "art and stories"— Rosselli occasionally employs quotation marks to stress a particular expression, whether for emphasis or to mark a cultural allusion whose origin is sometimes difficult to trace. This is the case for *"arte e storie."* As for *"in panne,"* the reason for the use of quotation marks may be that *panne* is a word of French origin—although in similar cases, Rosselli would normally use italics. In English, *stranded* doesn't require quotes, but we decided to leave them for consistency.

Bibliography

Agosti, Stefano. "La competenza associativa di Amelia Rosselli." In *Poesia Italiana e contemporanea. Saggi e interventi*, 133–51. Milan: Bompiani, 1995.

Montale, Eugenio. *L'opera in versi*. Turin: Einaudi, 1981.

Paris, Renzo. *Miss Rosselli*. Vicenza: Neri Pozza, 2020.

Pasolini, Pier Paolo. "A Note on Amelia Rosselli." In Amelia Rosselli, *War Variations*, translated by Lucia Re and Paul Vangelisti, 378–82. Los Angeles: Green Integer, 2005.

Petrarch, Francesco. *Petrarch's Lyric Poems. The* Rime sparse *and Other Lyrics*, translated by Robert M. Durling. Cambridge, MA, and London: Harvard University Press, 1999 [1976].

Rosselli, Amelia. *L'opera poetica*. Edited by Stefano Giovannuzzi. Milan: Mondadori, 2012.

—. "Metrical Spaces." In *Locomotrix. Selected Poetry and Prose of Amelia Rosselli*. Edited and translated by Jennifer Scappettone, 247–52. Chicago: Chicago University Press, 2012.

—. *È vostra la vita che ho perso. Conversazioni e interviste 1964-1995*. Edited by Monica Venturini and Silvia De March. Florence: Le Lettere, 2010.

—. *La furia dei venti contrari. Variazioni Amelia Rosselli con testi inediti e dispersi dell'autrice*. Edited by Andrea Cortellessa. Florence: Le Lettere, 2007.

—. *Una scrittura plurale. Saggi e interventi critici*. Novara: Interlinea, 2004.

Editions available in English by Amelia Rosselli

War Variations. Translated by Lucia Re and Paul Vangelisti. Los Angeles: Green Integer, 2005 [reprinted Los Angeles: Otis Books|Seismicity Editions, 2016].

The Dragonfly. A Selection of Poems. 1953–1981. Translated by Deborah Woodard and Giuseppe Leporace. New York: Chelsea Editions, 2009.

Locomotrix. Selected Poetry and Prose of Amelia Rosselli. Edited and translated by Jennifer Scappettone. Chicago: Chicago University Press, 2012.

Impromptu. A Trilingual Edition. Edited by Gian Maria Annovi. Translated by Gian Maria Annovi, Diana Thow, and Jean-Charles Vegliante. Toronto, Buffalo and Lancaster, UK: Guernica Editions, 2014.

Hospital Series. Translated by Deborah Woodard, Roberta Antognini, and Giuseppe Leporace. New York: New Directions, 2015.

Hospital Series. Translated by Diana Thow. Los Angeles: Otis Books|Seismicity Editions, 2017.

Obtuse Diary. Translated by Deborah Woodard, Roberta Antognini, and Dario De Pasquale. Seattle: Entre Rios Books, 2018.

The Dragonfly. Translated by Roberta Antognini and Deborah Woodard. Seattle: Entre Rios Books, 2023.

Sleep. Introduction by Barry Schwabsky. New York: New York Review Books, 2023.

Notes Scattered and Lost. Translated by Roberta Antognini and Deborah Woodard. Seattle: Entre Rios Books, 2024.

Acknowledgments

Many thanks to the editors of the following journals in which earlier versions of these translation have appeared: *Action Books Blog, Annulet, Asymptote, ballast, Cordite Poetry Review, Ezra, Modern Poetry in Translation, Notre Dame Review,* and *World Poetry Review.*

Special thanks go to our editor, Matvei Yankelevich of World Poetry Books, for the care and attention given to our typescript by a publisher who continues to believe in the lasting power and value of poetry.

Grateful acknowledgment is made to Gruppo editoriale Mauri Spagnol for granting permission to publish this edition. Publication was made possible in part by a grant from The Mellon Career and Curricular Transitions Endowment Fund. We are grateful to Vassar College Research Committee for its support.

Amelia Rosselli in October 1991, photographed in the garden of Casa Italiana Zerilli-Marimò at New York University, on the occasion of the conference *The Disappearing Pheasant: Italian Poetry Today*. Courtesy of Casa Italiana Zerilli-Marimò, New York, NY.

Amelia Rosselli was born in Paris on March 28, 1930, to the British political activist Marion Cave and Carlo Rosselli, an antifascist Italian political leader and philosopher of Jewish descent. She was named after her grandmother, the distinguished suffragette and playwright, Amelia Pincherle Rosselli. After her father was assassinated in Paris by the Fascist secret service, the family moved to England and then to the United States, finding sanctuary among other Italian exiles in Larchmont, NY. In 1946, at the end of the war, Rosselli returned to Europe, staying briefly in Florence before moving to London to complete her studies. In 1948, she settled in Rome where she would spend the rest of her life. She translated Emily Dickinson and Sylvia Plath into Italian, and was an accomplished musicologist and musician, who played the violin, the piano, and the organ. Rosselli published eight collections of poetry: *War Variations* (1964), *Hospital Series* (1969), *Document (1966–1973)* (1976), *Impromptu* (1981), *First Writings (1952–1963)* (1980), *Notes Scattered and Lost (1966–1977)* (1983), *Obtuse Diary (1954–1968)* (1990), and *Sleep: Poems in English* (1992). Aside from one early collection, all of Rosselli's works have been translated into English. Rosselli died in Rome, taking her own life, on February 11, 1996.

Roberta Antognini and Deborah Woodard have published several collections of their translations of Amelia Rosselli: *Hospital Series, Obtuse Diary, The Dragonfly,* and *Notes Scattered and Lost.* **Roberta Antognini** is from Canton Ticino, Switzerland. She has a Laurea from the Università Cattolica di Milano, Italy, and a PhD from New York University. She is Associate Professor Emerita of Italian Studies at Vassar College, the author of a monograph on Petrarch, and co-editor of a collection of essays on Giorgio Bassani, whose collected poems she translated with Peter Robinson. **Deborah Woodard** studied with Charles Simic at the University of New Hampshire and has a PhD from the University of Washington. Her books include *Borrowed Tales* (Stockport Flats) and *No Finis: Triangle Testimonies, 1911* (Ravenna Press). She teaches at Hugo House in Seattle, Washington, and co-curates the reading series Margin Shift.

The image on the cover is based on one of a series of Amelia Rosselli's artworks in pencil, charcoal, and tempera on paper of various sizes and weights, made between September 1952 and March 1953. Ninety-nine of these works remain, preserved at the Centro Manoscritti of the University of Pavia. Some of them were exhibited in Florence in 1953 and again in Rome in 1962. Fifteen of these drawings and watercolors are reproduced in the book *La furia dei venti contrari*, edited by Andrea Cortellessa (Florence: Le Lettere, 2007), which includes an essay on Rosselli's artworks by Stefano Giovannuzzi.

This book was typeset in Zenon, a contemporary roman developed from analysis of Renaissance models. It was designed by Riccardo Olocco from 2013 to 2022 for Cooperativa Anonima Servizi Tipografici, Verona. The cover, designed by Andrew Bourne, features Futura Passata, designed by Joseph Miceli for AlfaType, Torino. Typesetting by Don't Look Now. Printed and bound in Lithuania by BALTO Print. Manufactured by Arctic Paper in Sweden, the paper in this book meets EU Ecolabel, Forest Stewardship Council, and Cradle to Cradle certification standards.

 WORLD POETRY

Marie-Noëlle Agniau
The Escapades
tr. Jesse Hover Amar

Nadia Anjuman
Smoke Drifts: Selected Poems
tr. Diana Arterian & Marina Omar

Jean-Paul Auxeméry
Selected Poems
tr. Nathaniel Tarn

Boethius
The Poems from On the Consolation of Philosophy
tr. Peter Glassgold

Maria Borio
Transparencies
tr. Danielle Pieratti

Astrid Cabral
Spotlight on the Word
tr. Alexis Levitin

Jeannette L. Clariond
Goddesses of Water
tr. Samantha Schnee

Jacques Darras
John Scotus Eriugena at Laon
tr. Richard Sieburth

Mario dell'Arco
Day Lasts Forever: Selected Poems
tr. Marc Alan Di Martino

Marie de Quatrebarbes
The Vitals
tr. Aiden Farrell

Olivia Elias
Chaos, Crossing
tr. Kareem James Abu-Zeid

Gastón Fernández
Apparent Breviary
tr. KM Cascia

Jerzy Ficowski
Everything I Don't Know
tr. Jennifer Grotz & Piotr Sommer
PEN AWARD FOR POETRY IN TRANSLATION

Antonio Gamoneda
Book of the Cold
tr. Katherine M. Hedeen & Víctor Rodríguez Núñez

Mireille Gansel
Soul House
tr. Joan Seliger Sidney

Óscar García Sierra
Houston, I'm the problem
tr. Carmen Yus Quintero

Phoebe Giannisi
Homerica
tr. Brian Sneeden

Zuzanna Ginczanka
On Centaurs & Other Poems
tr. Alex Braslavsky

Julien Gracq
Abounding Freedom
tr. Alice Yang

Leeladhar Jagoori
What of the Earth Was Saved
tr. Matt Reeck

Nakedness Is My End: Poems from the Greek Anthology
tr. Edmund Keeley

Birhan Keskin
Earthly Conditions: Selected Poems
tr. Öykü Tekten

Jazra Khaleed
The Light That Burns Us
ed. Karen Van Dyck

Judith Kiros
O
tr. Kira Josefsson

Dimitra Kotoula
The Slow Horizon That Breathes
tr. Maria Nazos

Maria Laina
Hers
tr. Karen Van Dyck

Maria Laina
Rose Fear
tr. Sarah McCann

Perrin Langda
A Few Microseconds on Earth
tr. Pauline Levy Valensi

Anna Malihon
Girl with a Bullet
tr. Olena Jennings

Afrizal Malna
Document Shredding Museum
tr. Daniel Owen

Joyce Mansour
In the Glittering Maw: Selected Poems
tr. C. Francis Fisher

Manuel Maples Arce
Stridentist Poems
tr. KM Cascia

Ennio Moltedo
Night
tr. Marguerite Feitlowitz

Meret Oppenheim
The Loveliest Vowel Empties: Collected Poems
tr. Kathleen Heil

Giovanni Pascoli
Last Dream
tr. Geoffrey Brock
RAIZISS/DE PALCHI TRANSLATION AWARD

Gabriel Pomerand
Saint Ghetto of the Loans
tr. Michael Kasper &
Bhamati Viswanathan

Liliana Ponce
Theory of the Voice and Dream
tr. Michael Martin Shea

Rainer Maria Rilke
Where the Paths Do Not Go
tr. Burton Pike

Amelia Rosselli
Document
tr. Roberta Antognini & Deborah Woodard

Elisabeth Rynell
Night Talks
tr. Rika Lesser

Waly Salomão
Border Fare
tr. Maryam Monalisa Gharavi

George Sarantaris
Abyss and Song: Selected Poems
tr. Pria Louka

George Seferis
Book of Exercises II
tr. Jennifer R. Kellogg

Seo Jung Hak
The Cheapest France in Town
tr. Megan Sungyoon

Ahmad Shamlou
Elegies of the Earth: Selected Poems
tr. Niloufar Talebi

Ardengo Soffici
Simultaneities & Lyric Chemisms
tr. Olivia E. Sears

Liesl Ujvary
Good & Safe
tr. Ann Cotten & Anna-Isabella Dinwoodie

Paul Verlaine
Before Wisdom: The Early Poems
tr. Keith Waldrop & K.A. Hays

Witold Wirpsza
Apotheosis of Music
tr. Frank L. Vigoda

Uljana Wolf
kochanie, today i bought bread
tr. Greg Nissan

Ye Lijun
My Mountain Country
tr. Fiona Sze-Lorrain

Verónica Zondek
Cold Fire
tr. Katherine Silver

Maria Laina
Rose Fear
tr. Sarah McCann

Perrin Langda
A Few Microseconds on Earth
tr. Pauline Levy Valensi

Anna Malihon
Girl with a Bullet
tr. Olena Jennings

Afrizal Malna
Document Shredding Museum
tr. Daniel Owen

Joyce Mansour
In the Glittering Maw: Selected Poems
tr. C. Francis Fisher

Manuel Maples Arce
Stridentist Poems
tr. KM Cascia

Ennio Moltedo
Night
tr. Marguerite Feitlowitz

Meret Oppenheim
The Loveliest Vowel Empties: Collected Poems
tr. Kathleen Heil

Giovanni Pascoli
Last Dream
tr. Geoffrey Brock
RAIZISS/DE PALCHI TRANSLATION AWARD

Gabriel Pomerand
Saint Ghetto of the Loans
tr. Michael Kasper &
Bhamati Viswanathan

Liliana Ponce
Theory of the Voice and Dream
tr. Michael Martin Shea

Rainer Maria Rilke
Where the Paths Do Not Go
tr. Burton Pike

Amelia Rosselli
Document
tr. Roberta Antognini & Deborah Woodard

Elisabeth Rynell
Night Talks
tr. Rika Lesser

Waly Salomão
Border Fare
tr. Maryam Monalisa Gharavi

George Sarantaris
Abyss and Song: Selected Poems
tr. Pria Louka

George Seferis
Book of Exercises II
tr. Jennifer R. Kellogg

Seo Jung Hak
The Cheapest France in Town
tr. Megan Sungyoon

Ahmad Shamlou
Elegies of the Earth: Selected Poems
tr. Niloufar Talebi

Ardengo Soffici
Simultaneities & Lyric Chemisms
tr. Olivia E. Sears

Liesl Ujvary
Good & Safe
tr. Ann Cotten & Anna-Isabella Dinwoodie

Paul Verlaine
Before Wisdom: The Early Poems
tr. Keith Waldrop & K.A. Hays

Witold Wirpsza
Apotheosis of Music
tr. Frank L. Vigoda

Uljana Wolf
kochanie, today i bought bread
tr. Greg Nissan

Ye Lijun
My Mountain Country
tr. Fiona Sze-Lorrain

Verónica Zondek
Cold Fire
tr. Katherine Silver